Cyber Security Toolkit

Other titles available from Law Society Publishing:

Anti-Bribery Toolkit
Amy Bell

Anti-Money Laundering Toolkit
Alison Matthews

COLPs Toolkit (2nd edn)
Michelle Garlick

Data Protection Toolkit
Alison Matthews

Financial Stability Toolkit
Peter Scott and Andy Poole

Titles from Law Society Publishing can be ordered from all good bookshops or direct (telephone 0370 850 1422, email **lawsociety@prolog.uk.com** or visit our online shop at **bookshop.lawsociety.org.uk**).

Cyber Security Toolkit

Peter Wright

The Law Society

ISBN-13: 978-1-78446-042-6

Published in 2016 by the Law Society
113 Chancery Lane, London WC2A 1PL

Typeset by Columns Design XML Ltd, Reading
Printed by Hobbs the Printers Ltd, Totton, Hants

The paper used for the text pages of this book is FSC® certified. FSC (the Forest Stewardship Council®) is an international network to promote responsible management of the world's forests.

FSC
www.fsc.org
MIX
Board from responsible sources
FSC® C020438

Contents

How to use this toolkit

This book is specifically designed for those engaged in law firm management. This includes practice managers, partners and directors. It deals with cyber security threats and management, and is written to make IT accessible to readers without an IT background. However, IT specialists who are either supplying law firms or working in-house at a law firm may find **Chapter 5** ('Legal and regulatory standards') worth a look as it will be of assistance when identifying the most appropriate IT and security solutions for a law firm.

This toolkit will also help in-house lawyers to get a feel for the sort of structures that they may need around them in their place of work to ensure that cyber security risks are properly identified and managed.

Many of the principles of good governance (and the examples of cyber security breaches and their consequences included in the toolkit) will apply not just to law firms but to any professional practice and indeed to the sound running of any business in the current cyber threat landscape.

There are a variety of reasons why you may be looking through this toolkit. To assist you in finding the right advice quickly, some common initial questions and the section most relevant to each query are listed on the next page. However, we would of course recommend reading the full text of the toolkit in due course.

Please note that the threats discussed and the best practice recommended are correct at the time of going to press in 2016. However, cyber security threats are evolving all the time, and for that reason this book should be supplemented with up-to-date advice on cyber security governance from the sources listed at the back of the book.

Peter Wright
April 2016

Question	Relevant section
General	
Is my firm at risk from a cyber security attack?	**Chapter 1**
How should my firm react to a cyber security breach?	**Chapter 10**
What are the laws and regulations in England and Wales dealing with cyber security?	**Chapter 5**
What are the possible consequences to my firm from a cyber security breach?	**Chapter 4**
Policies and procedures	
What is the best policy for my firm when disposing/destroying hardware and devices we no longer use or need?	**8.1.6**
How important is it to include a cyber security threat assessment along with all of the other periodic risk assessments my firm has to do?	**Chapter 2**
Do I have to use encryption for all personal and legally privileged communications? If so, to what standard?	**Annex 9D**
What verification protocols should my staff use to confirm client instructions received over the phone, and why is this important?	**Annex 2D**
Staff training	
Do I need to provide cyber security training to my staff? How often?	**Chapter 7**
Why is it important to train my staff on the use of social media?	**9.3.3**
How and when should I be assessing my staff on their cyber security knowledge?	**7.4**
Is it important to make my staff aware of all the legal and regulatory cyber security requirements that apply to the firm?	**Chapter 5**
How do my staff and I learn how to spot a phishing email?	**9.3.1**
Staff risks	
Should I allow my staff to undertake work-related activity on their own mobile devices?	**2.4.3**
What are the risks of working in public places (cafés, hotels, trains, etc.) on public or private WiFi networks?	**9.2**
What cyber security risks are posed by staff that are leaving the firm and how do I protect against these risks?	**3.1.3**

About the author

Peter Wright is a leading expert in data protection, cyber security and social media law. As managing director of DigitalLawUK, he advises clients from across the UK and North America and has a strong following in the creative and digital sector. DigitalLawUK is the only specialist law firm in the UK to provide advice solely on data protection, cyber security, social media law and e-commerce, advising corporate clients on the conduct of their business online.

Prior to opening his practice in 2014, he held positions with Shoosmiths LLP and Nabarro LLP and advised on the successful defence of a group litigation action with a total liability in excess of £16 billion. His work included reviewing more than 4.5 million files and the disclosure of more than 20,000 individual documents using advanced online document management systems. He has also advised the government on data protection and Freedom of Information Act matters. He is presently chair of the Law Society's Technology and Law Reference Group and is the Law Society Council Member for Yorkshire.

A sought-after speaker, Peter Wright has led seminars and given speeches at numerous organisations. Among them are the International Festival for Business, WordCamp conferences for WordPress developers, Chambers of Commerce and Oxford Innovation. He regularly speaks at events for the Law Society and also for practitioner groups; including the Commerce and Industry Group, the Small Firms Division, the Law Management Section and the Lawyers with Disabilities Division. He has presented internationally for the European Young Bar Association, the American Bar Association, the British Legal Technology Forum, London Law Expo and at the Cloud Law European Summit.

You can follow Peter on Twitter at @DigitalLawUK and follow his blog and download episodes of the DigitalLawUK podcast at **www.DigitalLawUK.com**.

Acknowledgements

I would like to thank the following people for their help and support during the past year while this book has come together:

Janet Noble, my publisher at the Law Society, for her boundless patience and enthusiasm throughout what became a longer process than I think either of us at first envisaged. Simon Alliott at Notary Training, who constantly reminded me of the challenges faced in smaller firms and arranged for me to meet so many practitioners at his events around the country, as well as reviewing the final draft. Keith Etherington, who provided some kind words of encouragement and also took a look at the final draft. Finally, to my long-suffering wife Heather who managed to keep me going when all seemed lost in the depths of winter and suggested a short stay in a yurt in Derbyshire away from phones, email and social media to get me refocused ... and also for reviewing several drafts and giving me plenty of ideas for more checklists, forms and templates on the way.

PART 1

Understanding cyber security

1 What is cyber risk?

The threat of cyber crime is a fact of life in all economic sectors. Solicitors and their clients are no exception. Many law firms have received bogus phone calls or fraudulent emails from scammers attempting to steal confidential data or money from client account. As holders of confidential information, data and money, firms of all sizes are attractive targets.

You may consider that the threat of cyber attack against your firm is minimal. If your firm has little or no IT, you are operating from hard copy files, sending and receiving letters, taking cheques to the bank to be paid in and using a typewriter, it is possible you are right: the risk of a cyber attack may be minimal but it still exists. Data about your firm is held online by the Solicitors Regulation Authority (SRA), in Find a Solicitor, by your bank, your insurer and your clients. They can all be hacked. The data could be used to call your office, impersonate your bank, identify a problem with your client account and persuade you to transfer funds. This happened to a sole practitioner in 2015, and it ruined their business and their career.

You may try to isolate yourself from computer networks but if you operate a business in England and Wales – or, indeed, any country in the world – in 2016 you are still at risk from cyber attack. Smaller firms may be at greater risk due to:

- fewer layers of protection;
- less in-house IT expertise;
- lower levels of awareness; and
- fewer cyber security policies.

Conversely, you could be a large commercial law firm, confident that your investment in IT systems, staff and regulatory management systems across multiple jurisdictions makes your firm as secure as it can be and at minimal risk of being compromised. The partners of one of the world's leading offshore law firms – Mossack Fonseca – probably thought that, right before they found themselves at the centre of one of the largest cyber security leaks in history. The data, which was downloaded from their server and leaked to the press, amounted to 2.6 terabytes, constituting over 11 million documents. Due to the high profile of their clients, the security breach led to a significant amount of bad publicity and the consequences for the firm appear grave.

Other companies that have recently been victims of cyber attack include Sony Pictures (see **3.1.4**), Perry Hay & Co (see **3.1.1**) and ACS:Law (see **3.2.5**). As these high-profile cases show, no firm should consider itself immune from cyber attack, or neglect its responsibility to maintain, and rigorously monitor, its cyber security systems.

It is essential to minimise the risks before the worst happens; therefore, it is also essential to understand the main cyber security threats that firms are facing.

2 Cyber risks within business structures

Cyber attack is a business risk. For every £5 earned by UK businesses £1 is earned online and this proportion is increasing. The trend towards online transactions increases risk as businesses communicate digitally with their customers, suppliers and advisers. Where financial institutions and other corporate entities are a target their professional advisers, including law firms, may represent a soft underbelly – a vulnerability in clients' cyber security defences.

This highlights the fact that cyber security cannot be regarded as just an internal IT issue. Organisations face multi-faceted cyber threats which cannot be consigned to their IT departments. Cyber defence involves organisations and people and is inherently complex.

This chapter discusses a broad range of issues that businesses, particularly professional practices like law firms, need to consider. It will also explore how you can identify and classify specific risks to your firm by undertaking a risk audit (see **Annex 2A**, the Risk Assessment Audit).

2.1 The size of your firm

2.1.1 Branch numbers

The number of offices that your firm operates from will help to determine the kind of IT network you need. A single-site office location may be able to operate a lean and effective network at minimal cost. The more locations that your business operates from, the greater the risk.

2.1.2 Employee numbers

Staff numbers will influence network design. Support staff often handle everything from accounts, HR and regulatory tasks through to digital dictation support and hard copy document production. The level of cooperative working involved in support staff assisting fee earners with delivering legal services generally demands the use of a network and shared drive space. While the benefits of collaboration may be clear firms should be aware that they are accompanied by cyber security risks.

More fee earners means an increase in data flowing into and around an organisation. It increases the number of people working beyond the office walls: visiting clients, attending court, meeting third parties, travelling and working remotely – on the train, in a café, or from home. Again, the cyber security risk will increase as a result of this.

2.2 WiFi

2.2.1 Office WiFi

Many small firms in particular use a WiFi network in their office for business related activity and fee earning. While this is flexible and easily allows the use of mobile devices including smartphones, tablets and laptops, it also opens up the risk of the network being targeted and accessed by an unauthorised third party.

Public WiFi networks cannot be considered secure because the integrity of the WiFi access point and the internet connection can be easily compromised, allowing criminals to intercept and read any data transmitted.

Mobile data services such as 4G should be used in preference to public WiFi wherever possible. Firms should consider using a virtual private network (VPN). A VPN is a private network that extends across a public network (or internet), thus enabling users to send and receive data across public networks but with the security of their private network. This means staff can make secure connections to the corporate intranet while outside the office. Staff should use this whenever connected to public WiFi, before doing anything else over the connection. While on a public WiFi network, staff should never install any updates to computer programs or access sensitive information, including online banking services.

In addition, using WiFi for day-to-day working actually delivers slightly slower network speeds than can be achieved using a hardwire cable, and the more people that are on the WiFi network, the slower the access will be.

Hence it is worth investing in hardwire access for your primary office-based system, reducing the risk of the network being accessed remotely. Don't forget that a WiFi signal can be easily accessed by those on the other side of walls or even 20–30 metres away from the wireless router.

Furthermore, if you do use WiFi, the network should be password enabled – requiring the entry of a password before any sort of access is permitted to the network. That password should of course be changed on a regular basis (see **9.1.2**).

2.2.2 Visitor WiFi

Many firms want to offer WiFi network to clients or visitors to the office. However, small firms can sometimes fall into the trap of offering clients access to the firm's own network via WiFi, allowing clients to connect to the same router and same network as that used by the staff, including fee earners. Opening the network in this way is a major risk and should not be permitted under any circumstances.

Why not? If the client's device remembers the login and password information for that network and that device is lost, it could be used by an unknown third party to access the network. Or that information could be stripped from the device and sold online, again allowing an unknown third party access to your network.

The consequences could range from confidential, legally privileged information being accessed and sold to malware (malicious software) being installed on the system or on devices and machines being used by staff. Access to the practice's network must be limited to staff only.

The solution is to have a separate ring-fenced WiFi network for guest use. This should still be secure and password protected. This password should also be changed on a regular basis to ensure security. As it is used solely by guests it should have the bonus of providing quick access, enhancing their perception of your firm.

2.3 Remote server access

To allow staff to work flexibly, law firms increasingly offer remote server access to staff working from home or other locations. This can make it easier for staff and fee earners in particular to respond quickly to clients, to turn work around more easily and to increase their overall productivity.

However, remote access can increase the vulnerability of your system to third-party attacks.

The risk increases if staff use third-party machines such as those in another office or shared workspace, or in internet cafés, stations, hotels and airports. Such machines could contain hidden software such as a 'key logger', which can capture the key strokes taken by users on a device including the passwords for email accounts and remote access servers. The risk is even higher if the member of staff uses the same password across multiple accounts.

This is *not* a reason to forego giving staff remote access to the firm's system. But it is a reason to ensure that it is done properly, with effective encryption, staff training and security measures in place.

Firms should familiarise themselves with cyber security measures that can be taken. Some will be more cost effective than others. Two- or even three-factor authentication should be considered, meaning additional information is required over and above the traditional login and password. Two-factor authentication involves something you *know* (for example a password) along with something you *have* (a token). Three-factor authentication adds something you *are* (a fingerprint reader or iris scanner). Anyone who uses online internet banking will be familiar with the small calculator-like devices issued by many of the high street banks to their customers; these provide an added layer of security via a code provided by the device that changes after a few seconds. A cheaper option provided by some systems is for a code to be sent via SMS to a previously agreed and secure mobile device used by the employee each time that they log in. A suitably secure method should be adopted by your firm, and staff trained in the reasons for the additional layers of security to ensure their compliance in the safe use and operation of the system.

2.4 Office mobile device use

To facilitate remote working by staff, most firms take one of two options, either providing their staff with a mobile device such as a smartphone, tablet or laptop, or providing access to their systems so that staff can use their own personal devices to access the firm's network. This includes allowing staff to access their work email accounts, contacts and calendar on their own personal mobile devices. Note that unauthorised personal devices should never be used for business purposes.

If you are Lexcel accredited, version 6 includes a module on security for the electronic storage of information.

It is essential to have a policy or protocol for the use of technology for remote working purposes and the risks posed by unencrypted devices, USB sticks and the use of personal phones, computers and tablets (see the Bring your own device (BYOD) protocol at **Annex 2C**).

2.4.1 Regular screening of apps installed on work-supplied devices

A wide range of apps can be downloaded to smartphones and mobile devices, from social media to social gaming and retail apps. However, not all of the hundreds of thousands of apps out there are as legitimate as they may seem. They may advertise a game or social network but they could have an ulterior motive; one rogue app developer in France was jailed as a result of an app he developed that, once installed, would embed in a device's operating system and wait for financial transactions to be made. By skimming a few cents from each transaction on each phone where the app was installed, he was able to siphon off over €100,000 before he was caught.

Meanwhile, some apps take far more information about the device and its user than is strictly necessary and send it back to the app developer. Some apps can access information about the device's location, the social media networks it's connected to, photos stored on it, emails, contacts, web browser histories and more.

The solution is to limit the type and number of apps that can be installed by staff on their work-related devices. Apps should be strictly for work-based activity and preferably installed by your firm's IT staff to ensure that they are legitimate apps. Any work-related device should have restrictions put in place to prevent the unauthorised downloading of any other apps.

2.4.2 Regular screening of the contents of work devices for malware

During the course of their use, mobile devices will download huge amounts of data. This could include cookies (text files containing small amounts of data relevant to a specific user of a website) and malware (trojan viruses, for example). It is essential that devices are regularly serviced and screened so that any malware can be removed, and to delete cookies to avoid a build-up of personal data.

2.4.3 BYOD use

There are several advantages to allowing staff to carry out work activity on their own mobile devices, for example:

- the cost of providing a device for the employee is reduced;
- staff may prefer to use just one device rather than have multiple personal and work-related devices to carry around;
- staff may wish to use equipment that is more up to date than that currently provided by your office;
- staff who are responsible for updating office/work social media accounts may prefer the ease of use afforded by doing this from their own personal devices.

However, there can be risks and mitigating measures should be put in place. For example:

- access to the device should be protected (e.g. requiring a password or some other proof of ID such as a fingerprint) and not, like the majority of mobile devices, left entirely unsecured, leading to possible unauthorised third-party access;
- mobile devices should use ad-blocking software to protect against the threat of being infected by malware during the course of internet browsing;
- consider having a centrally controlled system giving the IT department the ability to wipe lost or stolen devices remotely.

Your IT staff or IT provider should be checking all mobile devices used by staff for work purposes on a regular basis. They should be looking for any suspicious third-party apps or malware. They should be checking for any networks that have been logged on to, for any unauthorised access or downloads that may have occurred and ensuring the overall integrity and security of the device. Such checks should ideally be performed at least every three months.

2.5 Telephones and voicemail

It is essential that your firm has policies and procedures to minimise the risk of successful scams by fraudsters. Recent telephone scams have involved impersonations of bank staff, clients, beneficiaries and others. Everyone in the firm needs to be aware of techniques and strategies used by criminals and this should be reviewed regularly to keep everyone in the firm up to date.

The Law Society's advisory article: Practical Tips to Protect your Firm from Scams (9 February 2016), has some good advice on telephone usage; see also the Telephone fraud checklist at **Annex 2D**.

2.6 Cloud services

Cloud computing involves outsourcing data processing and storage to an external provider. It is becoming increasingly popular, and sensible cloud use can offer more protections for small- and medium-sized firms. It can also work out cheaper than direct data and program storage. It permits true mobile working with no need for data sticks or email transmission of files, both of which are key risks for data loss. There are, however, dangers in using cloud services (for further information see **8.1.4**). See also the Law Society's Practice Note: Cloud Computing (7 April 2014).

2.7 Case management systems

Case management systems are repositories of large volumes of confidential client data. They can hold everything from names, addresses and dates of birth to financial details, email addresses, phone numbers and social media contact information alongside particularly sensitive information such as copies of ID (passports, driving licences, etc.) or household billing information supplied as part of routine anti-fraud and money laundering processes. Some systems permit the storage of medical records, details of personal assets and investments and other sensitive personal data. Some fully integrated accounts and HR systems will also hold personal data relating to fee earners and other staff, including details of appraisals, salaries and disciplinary records. Such systems are an information treasure trove for cyber criminals.

2.8 Handling client money

According to Law Society research, apart from theft of data, the greatest risk to law firms is the theft of monies. Criminals try to persuade parties to a transaction (including conveyancing clients) that the recipient's account details have changed. Recent telephone scams have involved fraudsters:

- impersonating bank officials and requesting information regarding the security of client account;
- impersonating beneficiaries and instructing firms that the bank details for expected payments have changed (for example, in relation to conveyancing or pension payments); and
- informing a solicitor that one of their clients is a beneficiary of a substantial legacy and asking for fees/taxes/bank details in advance of sending more information or the release of funds.

For good practice see **Annex 2B**, the Verifying bank details checklist

2.9 Risk awareness summary

- Have clear policies and procedures in place for all office systems, including use of the cloud, telephones, WiFi and any mobile devices used off-site.
- Ensure that all staff understand the firm's cyber security policies and procedures and that they are confident in following the correct process when risks are identified.

- Keep up to date with the risks posed by fraudsters, including the latest techniques, by signing up to regular e-alerts from the Solicitors Regulation Authority (SRA), Financial Fraud Action UK and the Law Society.
- To increase your firm's awareness of cyber threats and how to combat them, the Law Society can sponsor firms to join the Cyber Security Information Sharing Partnership, a free service for sharing information. See **www.lawsociety.org.uk/support-services/practice-management/cyber-security** for further information.

Annex 2A

Risk assessment audit

Introduction

Traffic light risk

The purpose of the exercise is to identify and classify possible areas of cyber security risk. A traffic light system should be used to categorise risks and identify legal and regulatory compliance:

Green – no identifiable risk, compliant with legal and regulatory standards.
Amber – some possible risk identified, further investigation required.
Red – clear risk of data protection breach or non-compliance with legal and regulatory standards.

You should be able to identify whether an answer is green, amber or red having read through this toolkit. For any question where you do *not* know the answer, tick 'Don't know' – this is an instant *red* answer requiring urgent clarification.

IT hardware and servers

1. Where are your firm's servers located – in your office or externally in the cloud?

☐ (A) Internal office server(s)
Please go to Question 2.

☐ (C) Cloud based

☐ (B) Internal server(s) located at another office location

☐ (D) Other
Please state: __________

If you answered (B), how do your branch offices interact with the server(s) at the head office?

____

If you answered (C), where are your cloud servers located?

☐ (i) United Kingdom

☐ (iii) United States

☐ (ii) European Union

☐ (iv) Other
Please state: __________

2. Does your firm have a backup system for your data?

☐ (A) Yes ☐ (B) No *Please go to Question 3.* ☐ (C) Don't know *Please go to Question 3.*

If you answered (A), please detail your backup system:

____

3. Do staff in your firm use Dropbox or other freely available cloud-based solutions such as Google Drive to share documents? (Check for unauthorised use by any staff.)

☐ (A) Yes ☐ (B) No ☐ (C) Don't know

4. Does your firm's network enable USB ports?

☐ (A) Yes ☐ (B) No ☐ (C) Don't know

5. How does your firm share documents with partner organisations or clients?

☐ (A) Email
☐ (B) Data room
☐ (C) Shared server
☐ (D) Post
☐ (E) Other

Please state:

____

6. Is your firm's data (client records, firm contracts, sales records, etc.) encrypted?

☐ (A) Yes ☐ (B) No *Please go to Question 7.* ☐ (C) Don't know *Please go to Question 7.*

If you answered (A) Yes, to what standard?

☐ (i) 32-bit
☐ (ii) 64-bit
☐ (iii) 128-bit
☐ (iv) Other

Please state:

____

7. How is your firm's IT hardware destroyed?

☐ (A) External contractor
☐ (B) In-house
☐ (C) Other

Please state:

____

8. Does your firm have a list of websites that have restricted/limited access on office IT equipment?

☐ (A) Yes ☐ (B) No ☐ (C) Don't know

9.	**Does the company network limit access privileges through staff user profiles, so only key personnel can access personal data? (Personal data is defined as anything that allows you to identify an individual, so names, addresses, date of birth, ID, photos, video, audio recordings, etc.)**
	☐ (A) Yes ☐ (B) No ☐ (C) Don't know
10.	**Do you have an office WiFi network?**
	☐ (A) Yes ☐ (B) No ☐ (C) Don't know
11.	**Do you provide visitors to your office with WiFi connectivity or some other access to your network?**
	☐ (A) Yes ☐ (B) No ☐ (C) Don't know
12.	**Does your organisations use a virtual data room, an online workplace or online sharing?**
	☐ (A) Yes ☐ (B) No ☐ (C) Don't know

Communication

13.	**Where is your firm email hosted from?**	
	☐ (A) United Kingdom	☐ (D) Other
	☐ (B) European Union	*Please state*: ________________
	☐ (C) United States	☐ (E) Don't know
14.	**Does your firm use web-based email (e.g. Gmail or Outlook.com) for firm correspondence? (Check for unauthorised staff use.)**	
	☐ (A) Yes ☐ (B) No ☐ (C) Don't know	
15.	**Which supplier provides your firm email service (e.g. Microsoft, Rackspace, etc.)?**	
	________________________________	
16.	**Does your firm send personal data via email?**	
	☐ (A) Yes ☐ (B) No ☐ (C) Don't know	

17. Does your firm encrypt all your email as standard?

☐ (A) Yes ☐ (B) No ☐ (C) Don't know
Please go to Question 18.

If you answered (A) Yes, to what standard?

☐ (i) 32-bit
☐ (ii) 64-bit
☐ (iii) 128-bit
☐ (iv) Other
Please state:
____

If you answered (B) No, what solutions does your firm use to send personal, confidential or commercially sensitive data via email?

____

18. Does your firm use a digital phone system?

☐ (A) Yes ☐ (B) No ☐ (C) Don't know

19. Does your firm use video conferencing?

☐ (A) Yes ☐ (B) No
Please go to Question 20.
☐ (C) Don't know
Please go to Question 20.

If you answered (A) Yes, please state the name of your video conference provider:

____

20. Does your firm use Skype to make calls or communicate using instant messaging?

☐ (A) Yes ☐ (B) No
Please go to Question 21.
☐ (C) Don't know
Please go to Question 21.

If you answered (A) Yes, what is Skype used for?

☐ (i) Internal staff communications only (e.g. inter-office or remote working)
☐ (ii) External communication with third-party contractors
☐ (iii) External communication with clients
☐ (iv) Other
Please state:
____

Devices and remote working

21. Do you provide your staff with IT equipment including mobile devices such as smartphones, tablets and laptops?

☐ (A) Yes ☐ (B) No *Please go to Question 22.* ☐ (C) Don't know *Please go to Question 22.*

If you answered (A) Yes, is this equipment tested and encrypted?

☐ (i) Yes ☐ (ii) No ☐ (iii) Don't know

22. Does your firm allow your staff to carry out work duties on their own mobile devices and IT hardware (including desktops, laptops, tablets and smartphones)?

☐ (A) Yes ☐ (B) No ☐ (C) Don't know

23. Does your firm record phone calls made to and from the office?

☐ (A) Yes ☐ (B) No *Please go to Question 24.* ☐ (C) Don't know *Please go to Question 24.*

If you answered (A) Yes, please confirm where the recordings of phone calls are stored and how long they are kept for:

____

24. Does your firm have a hearing loop?

☐ (A) Yes ☐ (B) No *Please go to Question 25.* ☐ (C) Don't know *Please go to Question 25.*

If you answered (A) Yes, please confirm where any recordings from the hearing loop are stored and how long they are kept for:

____

25. Does your firm have a CCTV system?

☐ (A) Yes ☐ (B) No *Please go to Question 26.* ☐ (C) Don't know *Please go to Question 26.*

If you answered (A) Yes, please confirm where any recordings of video footage are stored and how long they are kept for:

____

Social media

26. Does your firm have any corporate social media accounts (e.g. a company Facebook page, LinkedIn page or Twitter account)?

☐ (A) Yes ☐ (B) No *Please go to Question 27.* ☐ (C) Don't know *Please go to Question 27.*

If you answered (A) Yes, who holds the login and password details to your corporate social media accounts?

____

27. Does your firm have a corporate social media policy?

☐ (A) Yes ☐ (B) No ☐ (C) Don't know

28. Do your firm auditors run a social media audit?

☐ (A) Yes ☐ (B) No ☐ (C) Don't know

Password security

29. Does your firm require staff to regularly change their passwords (including login details for any, case management systems, document management systems, client relationship management systems, accounts packages, IT hardware and any corporate social media accounts)?

☐ (A) Yes ☐ (B) No ☐ (C) Don't know

30. Does your firm have a password security policy?

☐ (A) Yes ☐ (B) No ☐ (C) Don't know

Security and integrity

31. Where are your firm's office(s) located?

☐ (A) No physical office presence in UK – remote and home-based working

☐ (B) Serviced office development

☐ (C) Private rented office accommodation

☐ (D) Private owned office accommodation

☐ (E) Other

Please state:

____

32. Do you have key fobs or limited access passes at your firm's office(s)?

☐ (A) Yes ☐ (B) No *Please go to Question 33.* ☐ (C) Don't know *Please go to Question 33.*

If you answered (A) Yes, who is responsible for distributing key fobs or access passes and for collecting them when staff leave the firm?

____

33. Do staff have to wear ID or lanyards?

☐ (A) Yes ☐ (B) No *Please go to Question 34.* ☐ (C) Don't know *Please go to Question 34.*

If you answered (A) Yes, who is responsible for distributing ID cards or lanyards and for collecting them when staff leave the firm?

____

34. Do visitors to the office(s) have to sign in using a register?

☐ (A) Yes ☐ (B) No *Please go to Question 35.* ☐ (C) Don't know *Please go to Question 35.*

If you answered (A) Yes, who is responsible for the upkeep of the register and where is it stored outside of office hours?

____

35. Have your firm's office cleaners been CRB checked?

☐ (A) Yes ☐ (B) No ☐ (C) Don't know

36. Have your firm's office security guards and/or night porters been CRB checked?

☐ (A) Yes ☐ (B) No ☐ (C) Don't know

37. Has your office maintenance manager been CRB checked?

☐ (A) Yes ☐ (B) No ☐ (C) Don't know

38. Is your office locked overnight?

☐ (A) Yes ☐ (B) No ☐ (C) Don't know

39. Is your office alarmed overnight?

☐ (A) Yes ☐ (B) No ☐ (C) Don't know

40. How many people have keys to your office? Please provide full names:

____

41. How many people know the alarm codes to your office? Please provide full names:

____

42. Do you use any external consultants (including lawyers, accountants, marketing, IT, etc.)?

☐ (A) Yes ☐ (B) No ☐ (C) Don't know

43. Do you work closely with any other partner organisations?

☐ (A) Yes ☐ (B) No ☐ (C) Don't know

44. Do you use an external professional training provider (e.g. IT, manual handling, compliance, anti-bribery, including Chamber of Commerce)?

☐ (A) Yes ☐ (B) No ☐ (C) Don't know

HR, payroll and contractors (including consultants)

45. Do your employees have contracts of employment?

☐ (A) Yes ☐ (B) No ☐ (C) Don't know

46. Do your staff work a notice period?

☐ (A) Yes

☐ (B) No
Please go to Question 47.

☐ (C) Don't know
Please go to Question 47.

If you answered (A) Yes:
Please detail the notice period policy:

____

During that notice period, is employee access to the system/network and any personal data or commercial/confidential data limited in any way?

☐ (i) Yes

☐ (ii) No
Please go to Question 47.

☐ (iii) Don't know
Please go to Question 47.

If you answered (i) Yes, please detail how access is limited:

____

47. Who handles your firm's payroll?

☐ (A) Internal accounts/HR department ☐ (B) Outsourced to accountant ☐ (C) Outsourced to other contractor

If you answered (A):
Do they use a specialist payroll or accounts package to process staff records and payroll data?

☐ (i) Yes ☐ (ii) No ☐ (iii) Don't know

If you answered (B) or (C):
How are your staff records/payroll data sent to the contractor that handles your payroll?

☐ (i) Email
☐ (ii) Encrypted email
☐ (iii) Online portal
☐ (iv) Delivered by hand by staff member
☐ (v) Collected by hand by payroll contractor
☐ (vi) Delivered by third-party courier
☐ (vii) Royal Mail
☐ (viii) Royal Mail Special Delivery
☐ (ix) Other
Please state: ______________
☐ (x) Don't know

48. Who handles your firm's HR records?

☐ (A) All handled internally
☐ (B) Handled internally but with specialist cloud software support
☐ (C) Outsourced to third party
☐ (D) Don't know

49. Do you have remote/digital dictation or admin support?

☐ (A) Yes ☐ (B) No ☐ (C) Don't know

50. Do you have third-party contractors regularly in your office (e.g. catering, security)?

☐ (A) Yes ☐ (B) No ☐ (C) Don't know

51. Do your staff have full unfettered internet access?

☐ (A) Yes
Please go to Question 52.
☐ (B) No
☐ (C) Don't know
Please go to Question 52.

If you answered (B) No, what policy is operated and what sites or type of sites are blocked (e.g. YouTube or social networks)?

____

52. Does your firm have an acceptable use internet policy?

☐ (A) Yes ☐ (B) No ☐ (C) Don't know

Cyber security training and ethos

53.	**Do your employees know how to handle cyber security?**
	☐ (A) Yes ☐ (B) No ☐ (C) Don't know
54.	**Do your employees know the risks and consequences of a cyber security breach?**
	☐ (A) Yes ☐ (B) No ☐ (C) Don't know
55.	**Have your employees signed confirmation that they have received and understood cyber security training?**
	☐ (A) Yes ☐ (B) No ☐ (C) Don't know
56.	**How often does your firm provide cyber security training to staff?**
	☐ (A) Every year ☐ (B) Every other year ☐ (C) Other *Please state policy*: ______________________
57.	**Do you have a cyber security policy (stand alone or as part of an employee handbook)?**
	☐ (A) Yes ☐ (B) No ☐ (C) Don't know
58.	**When was the last time your staff received cyber security training from an external and accredited provider?**
	☐ (A) On: [*dd/mm/yyyy*] from [*company name*] ☐ (B) Don't know
59.	**Does your firm run a cyber security audit regularly?**
	☐ (A) Yes ☐ (B) No ☐ (C) Don't know

Annex 2B

Verifying bank details checklist

- Ensure you provide your client account banking details to clients in a secure manner at the outset of a transaction. Consider providing client account details at a face-to-face meeting with the client or by letter (hard copy, not sent by email).
- Alternatively, or in addition, consider providing this information at the time the client receives your client care information, perhaps in a stand-alone document also warning clients to be aware of and alert to scams.
- Make clear to clients that your firm will not be changing its bank account details during the course of the transaction. As a contingency, clarify with the client the verification process that you will carry out if unforeseen circumstances make changing the bank account necessary.
- Consider including a warning phrase at the end of the email signature block of all members of staff. For example: 'Please be aware that we will not notify clients of changes to important business information, such as bank account details, by email'.
- Inform clients that if they receive any communications suggesting that the firm's bank account details have changed, they should contact the firm via the number on the firm's website or headed notepaper.
- Ask the client whether they intend to change their bank account details at any point during the transaction and discuss the checks you will both make to verify whether an instruction to change the account is genuine. For example, consider using security questions to which only the client would know the answer.
- Treat any instructions to change bank account or payment details with utmost caution, regardless of how much information the person asking for the change may know about you or a particular transaction. Confirm the instructions by telephone or ideally in person. Consider asking for original bank statements for the new account which you can copy and retain on the file once inspected.
- Consider requiring written (as opposed to email) authority for payments, to reduce the chances of fraud.
- Remember that banks are not obliged to check the name of the account holder when they receive electronic instructions for payment – only the account number and sort code – so check these carefully yourself before accepting or giving new instructions for payment.
- Faster Payments is a payment mechanism which enables payments (or batches of payments) of up to £250,000 to be processed instantly, 24 hours a day, seven days a week. This facility has been used by criminals to immediately move account monies stolen in a successful scam and to forward the funds onward to a third bank. This makes it more difficult for banks to freeze an account in time and to call back the stolen money. It is vital you are sure the recipient is genuine – particularly if you are paying someone for the first time or if the account details have changed since you last paid that person.

- If you use Faster Payments to send large-value payments as part of your business, it's a good idea to contact your bank or building society directly for further information, as most types of accounts have a daily limit on the total amount you can send in a single day.
- Beware of 'invoice fraud', where a criminal obtains details of a firm's suppliers (e.g. IT suppliers) and emails the finance department purportedly as the supplier asking for invoice remittances to be sent to a new bank.

Annex 2C

Bring your own device (BYOD) protocol

Best practice when using mobile devices (telephones, laptops, tablets, USB sticks, etc.) includes the following:

1. Unauthorised personal devices should never be used for business purposes. If you are Lexcel accredited, version 6 includes a module on security of electronic storage of information. If staff are permitted to use mobile devices, consider restricting access on them to essential data and systems only.
2. Ensure a good antivirus software package is installed, up to date and regularly used on all mobile devices.
3. A reputable malware detection and removal tool should be installed and regularly used on all desktops and laptops.
4. All devices should be scanned for malware at least once per week.
5. Remind staff that they should be mindful of their surroundings when using work phone or laptops in public areas, and ensure sensitive information cannot be seen or heard.
6. The use of public power points or USB ports to charge devices is not permitted – devices should be fully charged before leaving the home or office.
7. Mobile devices are not to be left unattended or unlocked while in public places.
8. Staff personal devices should be checked by firm IT staff to ensure no malicious apps are present.
9. All devices used for business purposes, in particular carrying business email accounts, diaries or address books, must automatically screen lock when not in use and require a six-figure code or fingerprint scan to unlock.
10. If points 1–9 above cannot be satisfactorily implemented to address security and privacy concerns, consider banning the private use of personal devices that contain, or can be used to access, personal and/or confidential data.

Annex 2D

Telephone fraud checklist

Receiving calls

- Treat with caution any unusual telephone calls purporting to be from a bank or related to your client account and online security. As with all sensitive data, do not give away any details relating to the firm, its employees and its clients.
- Have you or a colleague spoken to the caller or their organisation previously?
- Be suspicious of any call purporting to be from a bank, the police or any other official or company in a position of trust, telling you that something is wrong, that you need to transfer money, or asking for details of bank accounts, including personal identification numbers (PINs).
- Does the number on the caller display screen match the number the caller should be calling from?
- If they are calling regarding a financial transaction and asking you to take action, take details but call back using only phone numbers that have been previously verified as being correct.
- If they are calling to notify of 'fraud' or 'irregular activity' on one of the firm's accounts, take details only, take no direct action, end the call, and notify the firm's compliance officer for finance and administration (COFA).
- If they are a client, ask the client if they can hold while you end the call then call them back using existing client records – the client should be pleased as you will be relieving them of the cost of calling your office.
- Never give out any authentication or account details (including usernames, passwords or other details that can be used to log into networks or your bank accounts) over the phone (either verbally or by typing into your phone). The advice from the majority of banks is that banks will never call you to:
  - ask for your bank security information such as your password;
  - withdraw or transfer your money from your account to a new account for safekeeping; or
  - ask to undertake a transaction to protect money held by the firm from fraud.
- There is no such thing as a 'safe' account into which your bank would transfer funds to protect your account – your bank would simply disable your account if it was being attacked.
- Make sure you take additional steps to verify if you are at all uncertain. Even if you consider a call to be genuine, do not deal with the query there and then. Criminals also exploit telephony technology by keeping a line open for several minutes after you have terminated the call. They make it appear that the call has been disconnected but stay on the line, so that when you call back on what you believe is the genuine telephone number, you speak to one of the criminals.
- Alternatively, use a different phone line (not just a different extension) or a mobile phone to call them back on an independently verified number.
- Always allow incoming calls to clear once they have ended – make sure that the line is available and a dial tone can be clearly heard.

Calling out

- From where have you received the number that you are calling?
- Is the source of the number verified and trustworthy?
- Has the number been used before?
- Have colleagues dialled this number safely for business purposes previously?
- *Do not* call an incoming caller back using details that they provide during the unsolicited call.
- *Do not* take immediate action as the result of an unsolicited call, in particular any irrevocable financial transactions.

If you have concerns about a potential scam, report it to a senior member of staff immediately. The firm should then report the incident to the police, or ActionFraud (the national fraud and cyber crime reporting centre) on 0300 123 2040, and the SRA on 0345 850 0999.

Annex 2E

Cyber security policy

1. Person with overall responsibility

1.1 The person with overall responsibility for the cyber security policy is [*name and job title of COLP*]. The compliance officer for legal practice (COLP) is directly supported by the firm's cyber security officer: [*insert name and job title here*].

1.2 The following people are responsible for overall cyber security in their specified departments:

- [*name and job title*] for [*department*]
- [*name and job title*] for [*department*].

1.3 The members of the firm's cyber security working group are:

- [*name and job title*] (COLP)
- [*name and job title*](Cyber Security Officer)
- [*name and job title*]
- [*name and job title*]
- [*name and job title*].

2. General approach to cyber security

2.1 [*Name of practice*] is committed to the highest standards of cyber security.

2.2 The management team has introduced cyber security governance systems and secure IT to meet the practice's cyber security needs. We will seek to monitor and improve these systems on a continual basis.
The principal cyber security governance systems are:

1. Risk assessment audit
2. Verifying bank details checklist
3. Bring your own device (BYOD) protocol
4. Telephone fraud checklist
5. COLP cyber security action list
6. Periodic review – cyber security supplement
7. Website management policy
8. Electronic backup and recovery system checklist
9. Device destruction protocol
10. Internet access policy
11. Password security protocol
12. Email policy
13. Email and personal data encryption protocol
14. Remote working policy
15. Social media policy and pledge

Secure IT includes [*case management, intranet or storage systems, secure mobile devices, encrypted email, online client portal, etc.*].

2.3 Our staff recognise their individual and joint responsibility to follow relevant practices and procedures in order to maintain day-to-day excellence in managing the often sensitive personal, commercially confidential and legally privileged information entrusted to the practice by our clients, and to maintain the practice's own cyber security systems.

2.4 Staff will at all times do their best to ensure the security of any personal, commercially confidential and legally privileged information that is stored or transmitted using any of the firm's systems. They will seek to maintain a high level of cyber security in accordance with the processes and procedures relevant to their role.

3. The practice's cyber security structure

3.1 [*Name of practice*] carries out cyber security audits of the firm's systems, policies and wider cyber security governance on a [*frequency of audit*] basis. The last audit was carried out on [*date*].

3.2 Schedule 1 to this policy sets out the firm's cyber security IT systems

3.3 Schedule 2 to this policy sets out in full the cyber security policies and procedures adopted by the firm, along with additions to the firm's regulatory risk management mechanisms including the risk register, taken in order to protect the firm against both current, ongoing and future cyber security threats

4. Managing risks to cyber security

4.1 We have identified the following cyber security risks to the following categories of information assets, along with proposed countermeasures and the lead member of staff responsible. [*Insert or cross-reference to relevant cyber security passages from firm's risk register.*]

5. Cyber security governance

5.1 Every member of staff is responsible for the protection and security of information assets entrusted to them.

5.2 On joining, new staff will be given copies of the following policies, which they will be required to read and sign:

1. Risk assessment audit
2. Verifying bank details checklist
3. Bring your own device (BYOD) protocol
4. Telephone fraud checklist
5. COLP cyber security action list
6. Periodic review – cyber security supplement
7. Website management policy
8. Electronic backup and recovery system checklist
9. Device destruction protocol
10. Internet access policy
11. Password security protocol
12. Email policy
13. Email and personal data encryption protocol

14. Remote working policy
15. Social media policy and pledge

[*Insert other policies as required.*]

6. **Training**

6.1 New staff joining [*name of practice*] will be introduced to the cyber security policy of the practice as part of their induction programme. They will receive training in the cyber security processes and procedures relevant to their role within [*number of days*].

6.2 Staff moving between roles within the practice will receive training in the cyber security processes and procedures relevant to their new role [*prior to commencing the role*]/[*within* [*number of days*] *of starting the role*].

6.3 All staff will be alerted to changes in the practice's cyber security policy and to changes to any processes and procedures relevant to their current role. If necessary they will receive further training or guidance in new processes and procedures.

6.4 [*Name of practice*] will maintain a cyber security awareness programme that will remind all staff of their key obligations under the cyber security policy.

7. **Periodic review**

7.1 This policy will be reviewed periodically on [*date*] by [*name of relevant member in senior management team*] as part of the firm's regulatory periodic review system.

Note: It is advised that you include a schedule to this policy identifying the major systems and their functions, particularly for staff who do not currently use those systems but may need to at some point. In many organisations it is common for staff to hear about the '[ACRONYM] system' without appreciating its function as the main finance system or the library system, for example.

Schedule 1

Firm cyber security systems

[*List all cyber security systems, including any acronyms, and their functions.*]

Schedule 2

Firm cyber security governance

1. Risk assessment audit
2. Verifying bank details checklist
3. Bring your own device (BYOD) protocol
4. Telephone fraud checklist
5. Cyber security policy

6. Risk register supplement – example cyber security entries
7. File audit – cyber security supplement
8. COLP cyber security action list
9. Periodic review – cyber security supplement
10. IT security checklist – quick questions
11. Staff training checklist
12. Individual cyber security training log
13. Staff survey – cyber security risk assessment
14. Cyber security compliance questionnaire for law firm suppliers/contractors
15. Website management policy
16. Electronic backup and recovery system checklist
17. Device destruction protocol
18. Internet access policy
19. Password security protocol
20. Email policy
21. Email and personal data encryption protocol
22. Remote working policy
23. Social media policy
24. Social media pledge
25. Breach notification (staff)
26. Breach notification (client)
27. Reporting a cyber security breach checklist

[*Update list as your firm develops further cyber security governance.*]

3 Types of cyber attack

Some people might think cyber security is primarily about protection from hackers, but in reality the variety of potential security breaches is much broader than that. It is no longer the 1980s and the threats are not (necessarily) bored teenagers in their bedrooms. The threats can be automated, coordinated and increasingly well resourced – sometimes even state sponsored, as Sony Pictures in the United States found out in 2014 (see **3.1.4**).

This chapter explores the different types of cyber attacks that firms need to be aware of, defining the perpetrators' motivations and capabilities, as well as identifying the various risks that they present to your organisation.

3.1 Perpetrators of cyber crime

3.1.1 Cyber criminals

Cyber criminals are in fact just one of the distinct cyber security threats that an organisation is vulnerable to. The cyber criminal is stealing for gain, usually financial gain of some sort. Typical methods include hacking into an IT system to steal sensitive financial data, or hacking into an email system to change the destination of legitimate funds.

The conveyancing department at Perry Hay & Co experienced every law firm's worst nightmare in 2015 when a client called several days after a sale had completed wondering where their £333,000 sale proceeds were. Mystified, the file was checked and it was confirmed that the client had indeed been asked, via email, to confirm the account details for where the proceeds were to be sent. The client had simply hit 'reply' and supplied the sort code and account number. However, a second email was on the file amending the account details to a different account. While this was issued from the same email address, it had never been sent by the client. Cyber criminals (probably using technology that scanned thousands of emails for financial data like sort codes and account numbers) had seen the original message, hacked the client's email account and successfully diverted the sale proceeds to their own account. By the time the error was identified, the fraudsters had successfully withdrawn £62,000.

3.1.2 Hackers

A hacker will be motivated by ideological reasons to attack an organisation, as opposed to financial gain. Examples of hacker collectives that have perpetrated attacks include Lizard Squad, Anonymous and LulzSec. The widely publicised AshleyMadison.com hack in 2015 was perpetrated by a similarly shady group, the

Impact Team. AshleyMadison.com was a dating site that members paid to use for the purposes of initiating extramarital affairs. The hackers were able to access the confidential details of all of the site's paying users. This personal data, including email addresses, was dumped online, leading to the CEO having to resign.

Another example of a high-profile hack, but a little closer to home, is the attack on the British Pregnancy Advisory Service (BPAS). On their website, a contact form allowed users to send online queries to BPAS. BPAS would receive an email from the site outlining the query. However, unbeknownst to BPAS and even their web developer who had inherited their site from a previous contractor, the website recorded a copy of the enquiry and this continued to be stored on the website. This data was unencrypted and only covered with basic security. As a result, an anti-abortion campaigner was able to easily hack the website and access several thousand highly personal and confidential enquiries. The hacker was apprehended before he could post the personal data online; however, the ICO investigated the matter and issued a substantial monetary penalty notice against BPAS.

3.1.3 Insider threats

Malicious

The threat from an inside source is the most likely cyber security threat to your organisation. A malicious insider is a staff member who acts deliberately. Often a disaffected employee, this could be someone who is leaving or intending to leave the organisation. At a serious level a malicious insider could cause considerable damage. A staff member could access the organisation's data knowingly to find something of possible financial value or to access sensitive data and send it to a recipient who should not receive it. For example, an insider who is leaving may access commercially sensitive information such as winning pitch or bid information relating to a successful procurement tender and take this information with them to a new employer, who would be eager to learn your organisation's secrets and commercial advantages.

The Mossack Fonseca leak was most likely carried out by a member of their own staff who had access to the whole network. The perpetrator was able to access current and archived files belonging to those who were long deceased, and to download an immense volume of documents over a prolonged period of time. Whoever it was had a knowledge of multi-jurisdictional tax and regulatory law and knew exactly which documents would cause the maximum amount of embarrassment – to both the firm and their high-profile high net worth clients around the world. Such specialist knowledge most likely excludes the average hacker or hacking collective; it suggests one of their own staff with access to the whole system accessed a high volume of material over a period of many weeks and months. The system clearly did not pick up this unauthorised behaviour and no 'red light' was set off, alerting other staff members that a large volume of documents was being downloaded and removed from the office.

Law firms are particularly vulnerable to the risk of malicious insiders, given the preference for prolonged notice periods of three months or more. Gardening leave (even for comparatively junior fee earners) reduces this significant risk, as does limiting system access to fee earners once their notice has been given. It can be tempting to rely on restrictive covenants in employee contracts, but this is not appropriate given that many instances of cyber theft only come to light many months (or sometimes years) after the damage has been done.

Non-malicious

However, an innocent inside source can be almost as damaging. An innocent insider who is responsible for a cyber security breach won't even know that they have made a mistake until long after the event. These sorts of breaches occur when staff members' poor knowledge in the field of data protection and cyber security isn't sufficiently addressed with informative training and assessment.

For example, an insufficiently trained member of staff could:

- send the financial details of an estate to the wrong client;
- send confidential or personal data via unencrypted email or other insecure means;
- ask for client instructions over an insecure channel (see the example of Perry Hay & Co at **3.1.1**);
- open an .exe file sent as an email attachment, unwittingly exposing a firm to a phishing attack;
- connect a USB drive acquired from an insecure source to a business machine, allowing a third-party user to have full unfettered access to a network.

In its worst incarnation, the innocent insider unknowingly facilitates a cyber attack perpetrated by a third party without even knowing it.

3.1.4 State sponsored hacking

Increasingly complex cyber attacks are now being committed by nation states.

- Stuxnet (unconfirmed perpetrator but believed to be a US-Israeli collaboration)

  The Stuxnet attack was targeted at the Iranian nuclear programme. A malicious piece of software was released online from an unknown source, affecting tens of thousands of machines globally. It had the effect of slowing most machines down and affecting overall performance. However, when it found its way onto some very specific machines in Iran that had control of centrifuges, it accelerated those centrifuges to breaking point. The impact of this attack knocked Iran's nuclear programme back several years, in a far less public manner than air strikes would have.

- Free Syrian Army

  The most costly tweet in history (to date) was sent from the Twitter account of the Associated Press in 2013. The false message read 'Breaking News: Two Explosions in the White House and Barack Obama is injured'. The account had been hacked by the Free Syrian Army, and the tweet was removed from the account in less than an hour. However, in the intervening period there had been a rapid sale of shares in US corporations on Wall Street, causing the S&P 500 index to decline and wiping out $136 billion in stock value.

- North Korea

  Nation states can also attack private organisations, as Sony Pictures found when its email servers were attacked by the North Korean government in December 2014. The widespread circulation of emails from senior studio executives, containing what they had thought were personal comments that would never become public, led to mass resignations and irreparable damage to the studio and its business partnerships.

- Moroccanwolf

  Closer to home, the NHS website **www.tellingstories.nhs.uk** (which details patient experiences of illness and treatment) was hacked by an organisation calling itself Moroccanwolf and claiming to support ISIS.

As these examples show, well-resourced nations and terrorist organisations are willing and able to hack into websites and email servers to attack individuals or organisations that are seen as threats. Given the highly personal and confidential nature of legal advice, it is not far-fetched to assume that law firms are at risk from this type of attack.

Indeed, in April 2016 the Law Society Gazette reported on 48 top law firms – on both sides of the Atlantic – that had been hacked ('M&A hack attack on 48 elite law firms', Chloe Smith, *Law Society Gazette*, 4 April 2016, pp.1–2). This, included two Magic Circle firms. Flashpoint, a New York web security firm, confirmed that the hacker had been traced to Russia and that the hacks seemed to focus on a series of mergers and acquisitions, presumably so that the data could be used for insider dealing purposes. Law firms were specifically targeted as they aggregate such large volumes of information around mergers and acquisitions and also have less rigorous security than that used by the large banks and financial services institutions, making them an easier target. The perpetrator may not have been state sponsored but still presented a significant threat from a foreign jurisdiction to a series of high-value transactions and circumvented the security measures in place at a series of large law firms.

3.2 Common methods of cyber attack

Understanding the most common methods used by cyber criminals is vital for all organisations. The more techniques staff are aware of, the more likely they are to recognise and prevent cyber attack attempts.

3.2.1 Social media exploitation

Humans are the weak link in a business security system. Even seemingly innocuous information posted by staff on social media can publicise events such as corporate moves, mergers, acquisitions, etc. For example, staff may discuss changes such as a relocation or a move overseas.

Hackers may manipulate staff by impersonating a telecoms provider or IT support provider and persuading the user to provide login names and passwords. This sensitive data can then be used to hack into your corporate systems, or to target the organisation with other cyber security threats such as phishing or malware attacks.

Some attackers will exploit known IT system vulnerabilities (for example, a weakness in a common operating system such as Microsoft Windows) to gain access to a network. Some quite sophisticated tools that can be used to break into seemingly secure systems are freely available online – for those who know where to look. This is a particular risk if your firm has a 'Bring Your Own Device' (BYOD) policy which allows personal devices to be used for work purposes. These devices are more likely to have operating system vulnerabilities, so can be more easily attacked than corporate machines.

3.2.2 Remote access hacking

If a hacker can gain remote access to a system or server, then they will have pretty much unfettered access to that business's systems. A powerful example of this method is the attack suffered by Essential Travel, a UK-based travel agency who were hacked in 2012 (Essential Travel was a subsidiary of Think W3 Ltd (TW3), TW3 was in turn a subsidiary of Thomas Cook).

The hackers gained access to the business's server via an internal car parking system. This system ran on the same server as the online e-commerce platform, which processed large volumes of bookings containing personal data – including financial payment details.

The parking system was intended for internal, staff-only use and could be accessed online from a non-customer facing webpage; nevertheless, that page was publicly available and could be accessed online by anyone who knew where to look. The login page for the car parking system also contained a vulnerability that went unnoticed by the developers, TW3 or any of the normal users for over six years. However, in 2012 a hacker accessed the page and exploited that vulnerability, gaining access to the entire server – including the e-commerce platform, which contained six years' worth of payment transaction details as there had been no security checks or reviews in the intervening period.

As a result, the hacker was able to access a total of 1,163,996 credit and debit card records. While some of the data was encrypted, the encryption key was stored on the very same server, so the hacker was able to easily decrypt all of the payment details, including names, addresses, card numbers and expiry dates.

The Information Commissioner issued a fine of £150,000 against TW3 (as they were the data controller in this instance), stating that inadequate security measures had allowed more than a million customer records to be lost and that the data controller should have taken active steps to ensure the personal data they were responsible for was kept safe.

3.2.3 Phishing

Phishing is a term for any method used to con an individual into revealing personal or confidential information. It could be a seemingly legitimate email from a respected organisation, such as a bank or a tax authority, with a link or an attachment to a website. Commonly this will take the user to a counterfeit site that convincingly mimics the official website that the user is expecting. The site will invite the user to provide personal data such as the password to their online account, or banking information (account numbers, sort codes, online banking security information, etc.).

The counterfeit site may also attempt to install malware onto a user's machine. Attachments such as .xe files often install malware onto a system. Phishing emails from banks and other financial institutions are particularly common and increasingly sophisticated. Once the criminal has elicited the required information from the unsuspecting user, the data could be directly exploited by the criminal who has obtained it or sold on for malicious use.

3.2.4 Malware

Malware is an umbrella term referring to any type of *mal*icious soft*ware* that carries out hidden functions on a computer system. Some of the more common types of malware include:

- Worms

  Computer worms spread to other computers by exploiting vulnerabilities in networks to replicate themselves in as many devices as possible.

- Trojan horses

  Trojan horses are seemingly innocent applications with malicious codes that secretly do something else. Often, a trojan's hidden function is to create a 'backdoor' to your computer – i.e. create a vulnerability in a PC's defences that allows it to be remotely controlled.

- Spyware

  Spyware is any software that illicitly collects data and transmits it to a third party without the user's consent.

- Ransomware

  Ransomware is a particularly aggressive type of malware that blocks access to a system and then forces the user to pay a fee to regain control of their computer.

All firms should have dedicated software in operation on all platforms to monitor for, detect and disable malware.

One recent example of a malware attack is the 'Solicitors From Hell' hack, which installed ransomware onto various law firm's computers. Solicitors From Hell was a UK-based website that sought to extort money from law firms in return for removing baseless complaints about the firms from the website (many complaints weren't even from actual clients of the firms). The Law Society took legal action against the website and the individual behind it and the site was taken offline. However, the site held the email details of many firms on its servers; once it was offline the site was hacked and many of the law firms previously featured on the site received emails containing ransomware. Concerned recipients, remembering the difficulties caused by the website, opened the emails and clicked on the links that they contained. These links then installed ransomware onto their PCs, and the ransomware demanded that cash be transferred – otherwise important data would be deleted. Many firms, particularly small firms, found their entire IT networks were compromised as a result.

Basic technical cyber protection from malware is essential and organisations should implement robust malware protection on exposed computers. However, the best defence is to reduce opportunities for infection by ensuring all staff:

- are aware of the threats;
- can reduce the opportunities for a system to be infected; and
- have the ability to notice when malware is clearly in operation.

3.2.5 Distributed denial-of-service attacks

A distributed denial-of-service (DDOS) attack will exploit the way a system operates to force it to slow down, or fail completely. This is intended to expose other vulnerabilities in the system to the attacker and allow them to exploit any revealed weaknesses to gain access or data. Alternatively, a DDOS attack could be a way of distracting IT security from a more serious attack elsewhere on the system.

This could be done through sending multiple emails in such high volumes to a target system that it cannot cope with the sheer volume of traffic. As a result, it slows down or shuts down completely for its intended users.

To date, the most notable law firm to be attacked in this manner is ACS:Law. In 2010 the firm was targeted by hackers after it had aggressively pursued alleged perpetrators of illegal downloading and file sharing of music, writing to private individuals identified from records provided by internet service providers and demanding payments on behalf of music industry clients for having illegally accessed and stored recordings online.

The DDOS attack focused on their cloud-hosted case management system and managed to force the ACS:Law website offline for a few hours. During attempts to restore the website, a backup file of the whole website was exposed online. This was then accessed by hackers, who found it contained unencrypted company databases which enabled them to leak over 10,000 names and addresses of individuals who had received letters from ACS:Law.

The use of inappropriate systems by ACS:Law (they were hosting business data on a residential cloud package designed for personal use) led to a fine of £200,000 from the regulator, and the ICO was particularly scathing of ACS:Law in the monetary penalty notice, highlighting that as a law firm they should have been more aware of the law surrounding the storage and use of personal data and that as a result appropriate measures should have been taken.

3.2.6 Cloning

Cloning, as the name suggests, involves the duplication of devices. This includes device data such as contact lists and email accounts, but the primary aim of a cloning hack is to duplicate the device's unique identifying codes. Consequently, if a fee earner's mobile device were to be cloned a client could receive a call and the mobile number that they know and trust from their lawyer will show up on their phone, making them believe that a call or text is genuine. Similarly, a client could receive an email thinking it is from the firm when in fact it is from a cyber criminal.

Close control needs to be kept of any mobile device to prevent cloning; mobile devices should never be passed to an unauthorised individual to use and should not be allowed to be taken into another room or away from the primary user for any period of time, however brief.

Premium security solutions are also available and can be put in place to ensure the security of mobile devices. However, ensuring staff keep tight control over their devices will always be the best defence.

3.2.7 Bogus firms

A recent development has been the rise of bogus law firms that are not regulated entities. They pretend to provide legal services, such as conveyancing, and in some cases may take on unwitting clients drawn in by the promise of an unreasonably cheap service. They will then contact law firms, purporting to act for either real or imagined clients, and attempt to proceed to an exchange and completion before then absconding with any funds that have been transferred.

More than ever it remains crucial to identify the identity of clients on all sides of a transaction via valid ID before also verifying the validity of all law firms – checking their registration details on Find a Solicitor, or on the relevant database of any other applicable regulator. If reliable confirmation cannot be found, any further work on a transaction should cease and the firm's COLP should be notified so that they may take the appropriate action with the regulator.

To mitigate this particular risk there are some practical things you can do:

- search your firm's name on the internet from time to time, since that might bring up a false office (it may be worth considering doing the same with the names of some of your partners or staff);
- use the Law Society's Find a Solicitor service (**solicitors.lawsociety.org.uk**) to check the details for your firm and individual staff members in case someone has misused your name to set up a false office;
- always check the website of a purported law firm. Is it properly compliant? Does it refer to being authorised and regulated by the Solicitors Regulation Authority (SRA) on its homepage? Does it refer to its regulatory structure elsewhere on the site? Are the contact details present? Bogus sites from bogus firms often forget these basics. However, they *can* appear very convincing and in some cases pictures of staff and offices have been lifted wholesale from other genuine law firm websites;
- be alert to suspicious incidents, such as transactions that others seem to think your firm is dealing with when you are not;
- look out for alerts and warnings on the SRA website about bogus firms.

The easiest way to attack an organisation is through its people, and that is what unifies all of the threats outlined above. All staff members must be aware of the threats and play a vigilant part in the firm's cyber security defences.

3.3 Risk awareness summary

Ultimately the risks outlined in this chapter are just the tip of the iceberg. Both the range and the complexity of cyber threats facing law firms are increasing; your firm's risk register needs to be regularly updated to take account of this (see **Annex 6A**) so that effective countermeasures can be put in place. They don't necessarily have to be expensive or time-consuming strategies – it could simply be a matter of revising and updating practices and introducing regular staff training. The first and most important stage is recognising the risks to the organisation and planning for the worst, while of course always hoping for the best.

Consider the following countermeasures:

- Protect your networks against internal and external attacks by restricting access and monitoring and testing security controls.
- Produce policies to control staff access to removable media (e.g. disks and USB drives) and portable devices.
- Encrypt any information stored on a remote provider, removable media or a portable device.
- Manage staff user privileges with regard to email, social media and networks.
- Ensure the firm's malware protection is up to date.
- Plan for worst-case scenarios and train staff to be vigilant.
- Establish an effective governance regime and maintain partner and staff engagement.

4 The impact of a cyber security breach

The full consequences of a cyber security breach may not be fully appreciated by managers in organisations that have suffered such attacks. This was sharply illustrated by the remarks I heard recently from a partner who, when addressing a room full of fellow solicitors, sought to identify with his audience by confirming that his firm had recently fallen victim to a cyber security breach. He described how his firm had lost £300,000 from its client account. However, he was relatively sanguine about the whole affair as his firm's professional indemnity insurance (PII) had covered the loss, and he regarded the matter as being concluded as a result. Yet one direct consequence that the partner didn't take into account was that his firm would face a significantly larger PII premium when the renewal date came around (see **4.3.4** for more on this). The following chapter explores various other negative effects a cyber security breach may have and how to mitigate those repercussions.

4.1 Overview of repercussions

Although cyber attacks can be devastating and costly in both structural and financial terms, the impact is equally damaging to the business's reputation and to relationships with clients. The consequences of a cyber security breach can include:

- loss of existing clients
- loss of future clients
- loss of reputation
- negative news coverage
- negative search engine results
- claims for professional negligence
- partner resignations
- difficulty in recruiting partners
- staff resignations
- difficulty in recruiting staff
- loss of third parties and suppliers
- effect on credit rating
- loss of financing with banks and lenders
- increase in PII premium
- difficulty in obtaining future cyber security insurance
- difficulty in finding new investors (if organisation is an alternative business structure (ABS))
- loss of existing investors (if organisation is an ABS)
- effect on AIM listing or potential AIM listing (if organisation is an ABS)
- an ICO investigation.

4.2 Regulatory actions

4.2.1 Action by the Information Commissioner's Office

Any breach should be reported to the Information Commissioner's Office (ICO). There is no time limit within which data protection breaches should be reported, but it is certainly better to self-report an incident to the regulator in plenty of time. This report should state:

- what happened;
- whether any existing governance was either not adhered to or had broken down; and
- what corrective measures were taken (e.g. increased security, improved systems or staff training).

In many instances, provided the spirit of the Data Protection Act (DPA) 1998 and its own regulatory guidance have been followed, the ICO will take no further action. Nevertheless, in the event of a breach it is preferable for an organisation to explain the circumstances precisely and voluntarily, rather than be reported to the ICO by an individual whose data has been affected.

Ultimately the ICO can fine organisations up to half a million pounds for serious breaches of the Data Protection Act.

If the Commissioner intends to issue a monetary penalty notice he will first serve a 'notice of intent'. This will specify the proposed amount of the penalty and the period within which the recipient can make written representations to the Commissioner. This period must be a reasonable period and must not be less than 21 days, beginning from the first day after the date of service of the notice of intent.

If the Commissioner proposes to vary the amount of the monetary penalty, then he must issue a variation notice which identifies the monetary penalty notice concerned, specifies how the notice is to be varied; and specifies the date on which the variation is to take effect.

A data controller or person on whom a variation notice or monetary penalty notice is served may appeal to the First-tier Tribunal (Information Rights) against that notice and/or the amount of the penalty specified in the notice.

To give a clearer picture of the ICO's decision-making and penalty levels, some previous cases are outlined below.

1. Bloomsbury Patient Network

   The ICO fined the Bloomsbury Patient Network £250 after it inadvertently revealed the identities of HIV patients through an email error. The network, which offers support to patients, emailed a newsletter to 200 patients and entered the entire list of email addresses in the 'to' field rather than the 'bcc' field – meaning confidential email addresses were revealed to every recipient of the e-newsletter.

For more details see **ico.org.uk/media/action-weve-taken/mpns/1560365/bloomsbury-patient-network-monetary-penalty-notice.pdf.**

2. Crown Prosecution Service

   The Crown Prosecution Service was fined £200,000 after laptops containing videos of police interviews were stolen from a contractor's private film studio.

   For more details see **ico.org.uk/media/action-weve-taken/mpns/1560074/crown-prosecution-service-monetary-penalty-notice.pdf.**

3. Worldview

   The hotel booking website, Worldview Limited, was fined £7,500 following a serious data breach where a vulnerability on the company's site allowed attackers to access the full payment card details of 3,814 customers.

   For more details see **3.1.2** and **ico.org.uk/media/action-weve-taken/mpns/1042093/worldview-limited-monetary-penalty-notice.pdf.**

4. TW3

   Online travel firm TW3 was fined £150,000 after it was hacked and users' personal data was leaked.

   For more details see **3.2.2** and **ico.org.uk/media/action-weve-taken/mpns/2659/think-w3-limited-monetary-penalty.pdf.**

5. British Pregnancy Advisory Service

   The British Pregnancy Advice Service was fined £200,000 for serious data protection breaches that led to a hacker accessing, and threatening to publish, thousands of names of people who sought advice on abortion, pregnancy and contraception.

   For more details see **3.1.2** and **ico.org.uk/about-the-ico/news-and-events/news-and-blogs/2014/03/british-pregnancy-advice-service-fined-200-000.**

6. ACS:Law

   ACS:Law was fined £200,00 for inappropriately storing unencrypted personal data, which meant that a hacker was able to access and leak over 10,000 names and addresses of individuals.

   For more details see **3.2.5.**

7. Ealing and Hounslow Councils

   Ealing Council was fined £80,000 for failing to encrypt laptops used for working from home. Two unencrypted laptops were stolen from a out-of-hours worker's home; both laptops contained sensitive data. Ealing's data protection policy stated that the laptops should have been encrypted, but no checks or reviews were carried out to ensure staff working from home were following this policy.

Hounslow Council was fined £70,000 in the same case, as they subcontracted out-of-hours work to Ealing Council, yet Hounslow had no procedure in place for monitoring whether the third-party contractors were DPA 1998 compliant.

8. Brighton and Sussex University Hospitals NHS Trust

   This NHS trust was fined £325,000 for failing to safely destroy hard drives. A hospital contractor used a subcontractor to destroy the drives for free. Only basic checks were carried out against the subcontractor, who was allowed on-site unaccompanied, and only provided one general certificate of destruction instead of individual certificates for each device. The hard drives were found for sale on eBay and still contained easily accessible medical records. There were no audit trails and no way of confirming what volume of data had been removed from the hospital sites.

4.2.2 The SRA and the FCA

A cyber security breach is likely to be a matter that should be reported to the Solicitors Regulation Authority (SRA) as a material breach. The SRA requires solicitors and law firms generally to have systems in place – both physically and electronically – to mitigate risks to client confidentiality. Risks like cyber attacks should be listed and categorised in a firm's risk register and appropriate steps taken to minimise those risks. If existing governance measures have been found wanting, or more robust steps are required, this should be identified and should form part of the breach reporting process to the SRA. Any funds stolen from a client account will be a breach of the SRA Accounts Rules because the rules impose absolute liability regardless of personal fault. Inform the SRA on 0121 329 6827 or email fraud@sra.org.uk.

Depending on the type of data lost, it may be necessary to report the breach to the Financial Conduct Authority (FCA), particularly if the compromised information involved financial details, affected a financial transaction or was related to a financial transaction. This could include not just data relating to an individual's bank account or credit card, but information relating to a house purchase, a company acquisition, merger or restructuring, or a cross-border transaction. Estate information such as the details of an individual's financial assets and holdings, tax arrangements or liabilities could also fall within the remit of the FCA.

4.2.3 Notifying the data subject

The data subject (i.e. the individual whom the data is about) should be notified as quickly as possible of any breach of their personal data in order to allow them to make arrangements to limit any possible losses. This could range from cancelling credit cards or spotting unauthorised transactions to taking security measures to address personal safety concerns.

When notifying a data subject about a data breach, it is important to include:

- the type of data that has been compromised;
- when the breach occurred;
- how it occurred;
- what steps have been taken to limit possible damage;
- what new measures have been put in place to ensure that it does not happen again;
- advice on who the data subject should contact for further assistance;
- confirmation that the ICO and any other appropriate regulator have been notified;
- details of any action that the regulator(s) may have indicated that they will take;
- a point of contact for the data subject to contact should they wish to follow up on any issue relating to this cyber security breach.

All individuals affected by a cyber security breach should be notified. If the nature of the breach means that specific individuals cannot be identified, it may be necessary to notify a range of possible data subjects who could have been affected.

4.3 Reputational loss

4.3.1 Personal reputational loss

Regrettably those responsible for a cyber security breach will rarely come out of the aftermath well. Should any individuals – no matter how senior or junior they are – be identified as being culpable in some way, their personal reputation will be tarnished. The implications of a cyber security breach can be so significant that the reputation of any individuals involved may not recover until a number of years after. Investigations following breaches can lead to professional negligence claims or fee earners at all levels being struck off.

In addition, partners may choose to leave a firm and take their client base and contacts with them, even if they or their department had nothing to do with the cause or consequences of a cyber security breach. The damage to the reputation of a firm caused by a cyber security breach could lead to an uncontrollable haemorrhaging of partners or other high-value staff who decide that their careers are best pursued in another organisation and now have the motivation to seek employment elsewhere.

4.3.2 Professional reputational loss

The reputation of a firm can be damaged too. Notification of data subjects and regulators can trigger coverage in the local or national press which can live on in web searches for years to come.

A cyber security leak could even affect the reputation of a law firm's clients. If a firm was offering a service such as outsourced HR management and consultancy (involving the management of staff HR records for a client), the client would remain as the data controller for that data, with the law firm acting as the processor. In the event of a cyber security breach within the law firm, the firm would be in the unenviable position of having to notify its client that the firm had been subject to a cyber security breach. However, the client organisation, as the data controller, would ultimately bear responsibility for the breach (despite the cyber breach occurring within the firm providing outsourced services) and would then have to notify any data subjects of the breach. Consequently, clients and partners could very quickly lose faith and confidence in a law firm following a cyber attack. It can take far longer to recover from the loss of reputation than to recover from the cyber attack itself.

4.3.3 Recruitment

The damage to the reputation of a firm can lead to difficulties in recruiting partners, fee earners and even trainees. This can be due to press coverage of a cyber security breach being the first thing that appears in a search online against a firm's name, leading potential new staff to consider working elsewhere as a result. Recruitment consultants could also choose to no longer secure staff for the firm, based on the disproportionate amount of time it may now take to persuade potential staff to join the firm when greater commissions can be earned from easily placing staff with other firms that are not such a hard sell.

4.3.4 Detrimental effect on the firm's PII premium

Cyber security is becoming a central issue for professional indemnity insurers, and firms will increasingly need to demonstrate what protection they have against cyber criminals before they are offered cover. In fact, many insurers are seeing potential cyber crime and fraud as among the top risks to law firms. Small firms are seen as particularly vulnerable as they may not have the IT systems and resources to prevent attacks. In the event of a serious breach, any reports made would further complicate the renewal of PII. PII is like car insurance – the fewer claims, the lower the premium. It is highly probable that any cyber security breach hinting at poor internal governance or controls could radically increase a PII premium for the following year.

4.3.5 Professional negligence and civil action

Possible legal action could be faced, from professional negligence claims to individual claims by those whose personal data has been affected, leading to a payout of £2,000–3,000 per individual claim. Even a relatively small data loss of records relating to a few hundred people could easily cause significant financial damage to a firm.

4.4 Financial repercussions

4.4.1 Damage to investment and market value

Law firms that are registered as ABSs or that are looking to merge with other practices can see a significant impact on their balance sheet as a result of a cyber security breach. A knock-on effect of the blow to the firm's reputation is a commensurate impact on the value of the business as a whole. Partners or directors could leave or be put off from joining, particularly if the business suffers any reduced turnover or profitability in the business accounts. Any institutional or private equity investors could be similarly dissuaded from investing in a law firm or ABS as a result.

4.4.2 Loss of time

Any fee earner who has experienced their IT system being unavailable for a day or more knows how critical IT access now is to the effective practice of law. Outages for more than a few hours can have a significant impact on fee earning.

Investigating a cyber security breach can lead to business critical deadlines being missed, leads not followed up, and opportunities lost. Key performance indicators such as chargeable time, fees and recorded time as a whole can be affected. A cyber security breach can lead to weekly, monthly and even annual targets being missed. Carefully planned growth and investment strategies can be derailed.

4.4.3 Loss of revenue

Existing clients could be lost, and future clients could be put off instructing the firm due to a poor reputation following a breach. Poor press coverage from a cyber security breach could persist for many years, polluting a firm's Google search results with negative articles.

4.4.4 IT upgrade costs

A new, more secure system could be required, which may require expenditure on hardware and case management systems, as well as online storage costs. Existing IT contracts may have to be terminated early, which could also carry a sizeable cost.

4.4.5 Credit rating and financial support

The firm's credit rating could be affected, which would have the knock-on effect of increasing borrowing costs across loans and overdrafts. Banks or lenders might withdraw their support for a firm, or certainly be put off from providing any additional support, which could be difficult for a firm already experiencing a downturn as a result of a cyber security breach.

4.5 Impact awareness summary

- Make sure you and your managing staff understand the possible repercussions of a cyber security attack, to avoid any possible complacency in the organisation.
- Identify the most likely repercussions for your organisation and develop a plan to respond to as well as prevent them.
- Ensure that your organisation's risk register records cyber security risks along with mitigating countermeasures.

PART II

Mitigating cyber security risks

5 Legal and regulatory standards

5.1 Legislation

Protecting the data you manage from cyber threats is a legal requirement under existing legislation, including the following.

5.1.1 Data Protection Act 1998

All organisations processing personal data, including law firms and legal businesses, must already comply with the Data Protection Act (DPA) 1998. Failure to do so can lead to a range of criminal and regulatory sanctions, including financial penalties and reputational damage. Following good practice and procedure in relation to handling confidential information and personal data will help firms to protect themselves from cyber attack. Businesses and staff are responsible for security, compliance and governance of data. The role of the individual is important in meeting these requirements.

Data protection is more than just cyber security and much of DPA 1998 is concerned with fair and lawful processing of personal data. However, Principles 7 and 8 of DPA 1998 are highly relevant to cyber security:

> 7. Appropriate technical and organisational measures shall be taken against unauthorised or unlawful processing of personal data and against accidental loss or destruction of, or damage to, personal data.
>
> 8. Personal data shall not be transferred to a country or territory outside the European Economic Area [EEA] unless that country or territory ensures an adequate level of protection for the rights and freedoms of data subjects in relation to the processing of personal data.

Principle 7 places a clear obligation on data controllers like law firms to take appropriate steps to protect personal data. Ignorance of current standards, common threats, obvious risks and best practice is no defence. The Information Commissioner's Office (ICO) has also in the past held lawyers to a higher standard of care than other business owners. Andrew Crossley, trading as ACS:Law, found that he was held to a higher standard when his law firm's cloud-based server was hacked. The ICO felt he should have been fully aware of DPA 1998 and the regulatory risks that he was taking in moving his firm's server entirely onto the cloud, onto what turned out to be an unsuitable platform that was not fit for business use (see 3.2.5 for more information).

Principle 8 is concerned chiefly with data transmission and data residency. Given the global nature of many law firms and the global nature of business through e-commerce, law firms need to ensure that personal data under the firm's control does not leave the EEA unless suitable security measures are in place. This can be a problem for multinational firms with offices in multiple jurisdictions (for example, a London-based firm with another office in New York). Up until October 2015 personal data could be exported from the EEA to the US under the 'safe harbour' agreement that guaranteed sufficient security standards. However, on 6 October 2015, in *Schrems* v. *Data Protection Commissioner* (Case C-362/14, EU:C:2015:650), the Court of Justice of the European Union ruled that the safe harbour agreement was no longer valid.

The EU and US have subsequently agreed the EU-US Privacy Shield to permit the transmission of personal data across the Atlantic, with the system set to become active in 2016. However, like the safe harbour agreement, it remains open to legal challenge; firms should avoid processing personal data outside the EEA wherever possible, ideally keeping their personal data, along with any commercially sensitive, confidential or legally privileged data in UK-domiciled servers to put regulatory compliance beyond doubt.

Law firms constitute data controllers under DPA 1998 and must be registered as such with the ICO. Failure to have registered or to annually renew ICO registration is a criminal offence and can lead to a significant fine.

5.1.2 General data protection regulation

Firms should be aware of the General Data Protection Regulation (Regulation (EU) 2016/679) (GDPR) that is due to come into force in 2018. Compliance with the GDPR will be necessary for all organisations wanting to trade within the EEA. Requirements will include:

- *mandatory notification* of cyber security breaches involving personal data to regulators and those affected by the breach; and
- the *right to be forgotten*, whereby a client could request the removal of all relevant information relating to their advice from a firm's system.

Penalties for non-compliance will include fines of up to four per cent of global turnover. Firms should ensure their full compliance with the GDPR prior to when it comes into force in all member states on 25 May 2018.

5.1.3 Companies Act 2006

If your firm is a limited company or an alternative business structure (ABS), the Companies Act (CA) 2006 will come into play. Furthermore, as a partnership or LLP there are generally duties and obligations that should be observed – your partners will be expected to follow and uphold similar standards.

Company directors have a duty to promote the success of the company by increasing its value, with regards to the interests of staff, suppliers, customers and shareholders. Part of this duty requires directors, under s.172 of CA 2006, to consider the impact of the company's operations on the wider community. Consequently, a failure by a company director to understand and reduce the company's cyber security risks could lead to a breach of this duty.

Company directors are also under a duty to exercise reasonable care, skill and diligence under s.174 of the Act, and a failure to adequately monitor and mitigate cyber security risks could breach that duty.

Furthermore it may not be sufficient to plead that such issues were beyond the skill and competence of the director; the standard to be applied on the company will take into account the online systems used and the breadth of data stored and used by the company.

5.1.4 Computer Misuse Act 1990

The Computer Misuse Act (CMA) 1990 creates offences associated with interfering with a computer, including hacking and using malware to breach computer systems. CMA 1990 makes unauthorised access to, or modification of, computer material unlawful.

Action point – Appointing a cyber security reporter

You mustn't become complacent in your efforts to protect your firm. Cyber security threats are evolving all the time. New laws and new regulatory requirements are regularly being introduced. To address this, an individual should be nominated to report back to the executive board, potentially on a weekly basis, on:

- news coverage of cyber security threats;
- industry best practice updates; and
- recommendations of steps to take to ensure both regulatory compliance and awareness of new threats to your system and security.

5.2 Regulatory standards

5.2.1 Solicitors Regulation Authority (SRA)

The SRA Principles 2011 place specific duties and responsibilities on those who own and run law firms. Principle 8 states that lawyers are required to:

> run your business or carry out your role in the business effectively and in accordance with proper governance and sound financial and risk management principles.

Given the financial consequences caused by the loss of both reputation and clients that can flow from a cyber security breach, the management of the risk presented by cyber security should be included within the good governance of a firm.

Under Principle 10, regulated firms are required to

> protect client money and assets.

Cyber crime presents one of the biggest risks to clients and their assets, especially their personal data and financial affairs.

Under outcome 4.1 of the SRA Code of Conduct 2011, law firms are required to

> keep the affairs of clients confidential unless disclosure is required or permitted by law or the client consents

and cyber crime presents a significant risk to the confidentiality that should be the norm in the successful operation of a law firm.

The Law Society has produced a very helpful Practice Note: Protecting Your Firm if You Fall Victim to a Scam (12 April 2016), that outlines clearly all your regulatory obligations.

5.2.2 ICO

DPA 1998 requires that all data controllers register with the ICO. The SRA expects law firms to be aware of this and to comply with DPA 1998 in full as a matter of course.

5.2.3 The Institute of Chartered Accountants in England and Wales (ICAEW)

The ICAEW Code of Ethics states that there must be compliance with applicable laws, regulations and standards and that the confidentiality of information must be maintained.

Professionals have a duty of care towards their organisations and their clients to ensure that they don't face consequences through a lack of professionalism or negligence. This includes protecting information that is important to the business.

5.2.4 The Financial Conduct Authority (FCA)

The FCA outlines responsibilities for organisations in the financial services sector. Furthermore, it is not just about organisations but also about individuals' duty to meet these responsibilities. Firms giving advice relating to any aspect of financial services (e.g. corporate, commercial or banking matters) need to pay particular heed to guidance issued by the FCA.

5.2.5 Accreditation standards

If your firm is accredited or certified under a quality standards scheme, there could be associated contractual requirements. Firms may follow standards from the International Organisation for Standardisation (ISO) (for example, ISO 9001 (quality management systems) or ISO 27001 (information security management)). Or your firm may be accredited by Lexcel, the Law Society's legal practice quality mark, which also requires compliance with DPA 1998.

The UK government has had a cyber security strategy since 2011 and there is an increasing drive for commercial suppliers to the public sector to conform to best practice in cyber security.

5.3 Regulatory summary

1. Your firm must register as a data controller with the ICO, to confirm regulatory compliance.
2. The SRA requires compliance with DPA 1998 and the ICO requires registration of data controllers to confirm that compliance.
3. You should know your firm's renewal date on the ICO Register of Data Protection Controllers (in 2016 the ICO began fining organisations for having not renewed their registration).
4. Nominate a member of staff to regularly report on new cyber security threats and best practice updates.

6 Implementing and monitoring cyber security policies

6.1 Cyber security risk management

We have looked at the threats to a firm, the types of attack that it could face, the range of consequences, legal obligations from a cyber security perspective and regulatory requirements.

So how do you minimise risk? Cyber attacks cannot be prevented completely but many threats can be countered with simple common sense steps. Security breaches are often most damaging when organisations and individuals are naive about the risks and do not have basic security measures in place. These measures are not necessarily IT-focused and do not have to be costly to implement. People are often the most important factor.

Risks can be mitigated by understanding what needs to be protected (covered in **Part I**), and then using this understanding to create policies that work for your firm. Essential areas that need to be addressed by these policies include:

- training employees and making them aware of the risks (see **Chapter 7**);
- putting in place cyber security controls and policies, with effective governance (see **Chapters 8–9**);
- having a resilient plan for cyber incident responses (see **Chapter 10**).

Before discussing how to structure policies for these specific aspects, this chapter gives a general overview of managing cyber risk as part of businesses risk and how to implement good governance.

6.2 Risk management at board-level

Too often boards are relying on their IT departments or third-party providers to securely protect the organisation without explicitly asking the IT staff to do so. If an organisation were to question the IT department or third-party provider about cyber security, the answer more often that not will be:

- the board did not tell us to do something about this so we have not done so; or
- we've made recommendations to the board but they have not approved the resources.

The bottom line is that boards need to take top-down responsibility for cyber security. Board members need to be educated about the risks and able to make reasoned decisions to approve appropriate measures to respond to the threats.

Board-level cyber security duties include:

- identifying the information to be protected and the associated risks;
- understanding the ethical, legal and regulatory requirements relevant to the business;
- establishing the policies and procedures to manage the risks, while balancing the benefits of taking risks and the potential costs;
- ensuring staff, contractors and suppliers are aware of and trained in the necessary policies and procedures;
- having a mechanism for managing and reporting cyber security incidents, so that lessons can be learned and remedial actions carried out when necessary;
- not transferring responsibility of risk through outsourcing (this is not legally permissible);
- establishing an effective governance structure and determining your level risk (as you would for any other risk);
- maintaining the board's engagement with cyber risk.

Action point – Maintaining a risk register

As an SRA-regulated entity, a law firm should have a risk register and use it to record all risks as well as the measures taken to manage and alleviate them. Cyber security is no different and there should be a supplement of the risk register devoted to cyber security risk (see **Annex 6A**, 'Risk register supplement – example cyber security entries').

The risk register should include the many and varied cyber security risks that are out there, but tailored to your firm. For example, if the firm handles large amounts of conveyancing work, and has large sums of money washing through the client account, this should be monitored and extra care taken when verifying client instructions regarding financial transactions. An awareness of the firm's specific cyber security vulnerabilities should run through your risk register.

Cyber security cannot be a focus for a few weeks then ignored for the next five years. Once governance arrangements are in place they should be monitored for effectiveness and, if necessary, modified as new security threats are identified. Management staff must continue to be advised of updates, must continue to engage in ensuring best practice runs throughout the organisation, and cannot be allowed to devolve responsibility – either by leaving it on the shoulders of a sole compliance officer for legal practice (COLP) to deal with or thinking that there is nothing else that needs to be done because there is a document sitting in a lever arch folder with the firm logo on it.

6.3 Delegated aspects of risk management

It is clearly important for firms to make sure all of their staff are trained in cyber security risks and prevention procedures. There are aspects of the day-to-day cyber security risk management that can and should be delegated, to optimise firm-wide protection. This section discusses some of the best practices when it comes to delegating or assigning these tasks.

6.3.1 Holding IT staff/providers to account

Knowing the right questions to ask IT staff and IT providers is essential. The decision makers in a law firm (including partners, directors, practice managers, administration managers and heads of department) must have a clear understanding of cyber security risks: how they could affect the firm, how they could affect different practice areas, how they could affect the way day-to-day work is undertaken, etc.. Only then will they have a level of understanding that enables them to ask sufficiently probing questions of IT staff and suppliers.

Decision makers do not necessarily need to have *technological* knowledge of cyber security. Being able to recall encryption standards, firewalls used, server locations, etc., while useful, will not develop the *logistical* understanding as to why these precautions are being taken, how a breach could impact a firm and consequently what questions need to be asked and the assurances that should be sought and recorded as part of the firm's risk management.

6.3.2 COLP actions and support

Staff need to be assigned the necessary tasks to keep the firm current and fully up to date in its cyber security awareness. It should not be a matter of delegating to the IT staff. The COLP is responsible (see **Annex 6C**, 'COLP cyber security action list', for a detailed breakdown of these responsibilities).

The COLP needs training and updating on cyber security issues, but also needs support. The COLP should work closely with the IT staff or IT provider to ensure, for example, that firewalls and anti-malware systems are both used and updated regularly. There should be a reporting or auditing system in place to ensure that all necessary tasks are undertaken regularly.

Senior management and partners cannot delegate the task of cyber security without understanding the risks to and responsibilities of the firm. All board-level staff should be able to give an appropriate level of support and direction. When IT staff come with a recommendation around cyber security they need to be listened to and understood; if they have a convincing case for a new solution, product or way of working, they need to be given the opportunity to state their case. Senior management must have a thorough understanding of the issues – technical, governance, regulatory and legal – in order to then make reasoned and effective decisions about IT staff's recommendations.

6.3.3 General staff

Every individual member of staff should:

- be aware of the potential cyber security risks involved in their day-to-day procedures;
- be aware of and adhere to the organisation's security practices;
- understand their personal responsibility for company and client information;
- understand their personal, legal and ethical responsibilities for protecting information;
- think before they act;
- be able to explain cyber security concepts to support external individuals (e.g. clients) in the protection of their own information.

For more details on responsibly supporting non-staff members with data protection, see **Annex 6B**, 'File audit – cyber security supplement'.

6.4 Monitoring

A law firm would not allow someone to walk off the street, have a search through their filing cabinets of archived files and then take a copy of anything that they wanted. Monitoring is necessary in order to prevent the online equivalent of the same thing. The threat from cyber security has necessitated the need for thorough levels of online monitoring and surveillance. This section outlines some of the ways this can be done.

The 2016 'Panama Papers' leak of 2.4 terrabytes of data from the law firm Mossack Fonseca typified the danger of a lax system of monitoring. The source of the leak was most likely one of their own employees. Over a prolonged period, an unknown number of individuals with access to the firm's case management system were able to access a huge number of files. These individuals probably had full access to the system; it's unlikely that this level of access was actually necessary for them to fulfil the obligations of their employment. For example, one set of papers referred to companies set up for the British prime minister's late father – around 10 years previously. The files relating to these companies were most likely closed and archived many years ago. However these files were accessed, corporate details were viewed and documents were downloaded. Documents left the firm (perhaps on a USB drive, or attached to an email or via a cloud-based system). The precise mechanics have yet to be confirmed, but the fact is that the law firm's systems failed to flag up the access to thousands of documents that simply should not have been opened, let alone downloaded or removed from the confines of their system.

Monitoring ensures that data is only accessed for the purpose for which it is being retained.

Many cyber security breaches are not identified until many weeks or months after they happened. During this time the data subjects of the personal or confidential data accessed could have been the victims of ensuing fraud, or the data could have been used to influence insider trading or for some other criminal purpose. This delay often happens if networks only receive cursory checks rather than a thorough review or audit identifying and remedying any breaches.

To enable your organisation to implement a monitoring regime, a cyber security file audit supplement for use alongside your existing file auditing procedure is provided as part of this toolkit (**Annex 6B**), along with a cyber security periodic review supplement (**Annex 6D**) to ensure that your regular periodic review takes account of cyber security matters. All firms and all systems are different and we anticipate that in due course you will be able to modify these supplements to take account of the specific threats faced by your organisation and the countermeasures taken as a result.

Action point – Sources of guidance

- The ICO remains an excellent source of regulatory guidance, and the ICO website should be regularly consulted for any new guidance. For example, in 2014 the ICO published a blog post confirming that there had been a large number of data security breaches within the legal profession that year. The blog post also included tips to help lawyers keep their information secure.
- The SRA has highlighted cyber crime as a priority risk for legal businesses and has some excellent advice and assistance on their website (**www.sra.org.uk/risk/outlook/priority-risks/cybercrime.page**).
- The Law Society offers useful Practice Notes as well as a new free online training course to help solicitors develop skills to protect their clients and themselves from cyber attacks (see **www.lawsociety.org.uk/support-services/practice-management/cyber-security**).

6.5 Risk management summary

- Have a monitoring system in place and produce supporting policies. Ensure that this is uniform across all networks and branches of the whole organisation.
- Obtain technical support to ensure that a breach can be identified effectively and follow-up steps taken.
- Continuously monitor all ICT systems and networks.
- Analyse logs for unusual activity that could indicate an attack.
- Keep your anti-malware systems installed and up to date.
- Make sure that you are using up-to-date, supported versions of the applications you use, including your operating system and browsers, and that you install patches from the vendor (e.g. Windows XP is no longer supported by Microsoft, but continues to be used by many organisations as a operating system).
- Make sure that you install any patches from the vendors of the applications you use (a patch is a piece of software designed to update, improve or fix a computer program).

Annex 6A

Risk register supplement – example cyber security entries

> **Note:** You must take account of other specific risks that could affect your firm and mitigate those risks accordingly.

Risk	Mitigation to be taken	To review	Reviewer/ responsibility
No clear cyber security governance structure	Cyber security policy in place with designated cyber security risk manager	Annually	COLP
Risk of affected parties and regulators not being notified of a cyber security breach; could lead to fine under EU General Data Protection Regulation	Clear action plan in place to manage a cyber security breach or incident, including reporting mechanism(s).	Annually	COLP
Staff unaware of firm's cyber security governance measures	Staff induction for all new staff to include cyber security training	Annually	COLP
Staff unsure of roles and responsibilities in event of cyber security breach	Key staff cyber security breach simulation	Every 6 months	COLP
Staff fail to grasp principles behind cyber security measures or apply measures to use of business IT systems	All staff to undertake cyber security assessment following training and reach 75% pass grade	Every 6 months	COLP
Staff unaware of new and developing cyber security threats, scams and frauds affecting law firms	Regular cyber security refresher training for *all* staff regardless of seniority	Every 6 months	COLP
Senior partners and staff circumventing cyber security measures having not attended cyber security training (e.g. using own Dropbox accounts for business matters)	Should staff miss two or more cyber security training sessions their system access will be severely limited until such time as training has been attended and assessment passed	Every 3 months	COLP
Risk from insider accessing network and downloading or taking client data, personal data or client confidential data	Background checks on staff, including occupational history, criminal records and academic and vocational qualifications to control risk from fraud	Every 6 months	COLP

Risk	Mitigation to be taken	To review	Reviewer/ responsibility
Staff taking client data, personal data or client confidential data with them to another firm when they leave	Access controls on system and unique user profiles to prevent and track any and all access to client and confidential records and when notice given by employee paying them notice and sending on gardening leave on day of resignation	Monthly	COLP
Abuse of system by staff	Unique accounts for each user, including each Administrator user and multiple additional Administrator controls	Every 6 months	COLP
Unable to identify unauthorised access or abuse of system	Regular user access reviews for abuse and anomalies	Every 3 months	COLP
Loss of personal data relating to clients leading to material breach and data protection breach	Customer/client ID authentication details stored using suitable security, encryption and obfuscation – explain process in full	Every 6 months	COLP
Unable to stop downloading of personal, client or confidential data to USB or email by internal users	Access system to restrict access to customer data with verification it has not been accessed, copied or downloaded except for specific tasks	Every 6 months	COLP
Interception of firm's email leading to firm emails being hacked	Encryption during transit of data sent electronically	Every 6 months	COLP
Mail or courier interception leading to data protection breach	Encryption during transit of data on USB flash drive, CD-ROM or DVD-ROM	Every 6 months	COLP
Risk of external hacker accessing system	Regular penetration testing; IT systems have most recent versions of antivirus software fitted with updates enabled; firewall(s) in place and updates enabled, external facing IP addresses subject to regular vulnerability tests	Every 6 months	COLP
IT system not up to date and vulnerable to hacker	Up-to-date operating system with updates enabled and up-to-date web browsers in use	Every 6 months	COLP
System back-up ineffective when needed	Test regularly for full and partial system restore	Every 3 months	COLP

Risk	**Mitigation to be taken**	**To review**	**Reviewer/ responsibility**
System back-up is not encrypted	Secure encrypted links used for data transfer if back-up is carried out online; if back-up is carried out on an external drive, ensure this is encrypted also	Every 3 months	COLP
System unable to back-up due to office being out of bounds	Physical offsite back-up used and regularly tested	Every 3 months	COLP
Mobile device used by external hacker to compromise system	All devices should be encrypted	Every 6 months	COLP
Mobile device lost by staff	Maintain full and accurate register of devices issued to staff	Every 3 months	COLP
Mobile device used by unauthorised user	Audit devices to ensure customer data is only accessible to those authorised to use it and that only staff with a genuine business reason for working on mobile devices are authorised to do so	Every 6 months	COLP
Staff using personal devices for business use	Have BYOD policy, systems and controls. Alternatively, *ban* use of personal devices for businesses activities	Annually	COLP
Unauthorised removal of client, confidential or personal data using media [inc. USB drive, etc.]	Only those with genuine business need authorised to remove personal data to media	Every 3 months	COLP
Loss of media containing client, confidential or personal data [inc USB drive, etc.]	Staff permitted to download client/personal data to media only so long as the media is securely encrypted and there is a genuine business need to do so. Destroy all data on removable media as soon as it is reasonably practicable	Every 3 months	COLP
Data stored in unsuitable jurisdiction and legal or regulatory breach as a result	Data held in UK or in a state covered by General Data Protection Regulation (Regulation (EU) 2016/679) (GDPR) or EU-US Privacy Shield	Every 6 months	COLP
Data transferred to unsuitable jurisdiction and legal or regulatory breach as a result	Data residency policy in place to ensure data held in UK or in a state covered by GDPR or EU-US Privacy Shield	Every 6 months	COLP

Risk	Mitigation to be taken	To review	Reviewer/ responsibility
Unauthorised access to areas storing client, personal or confidential data	Key fob, key pad or lock or other security measure in place on server room, filing cabinets, archives, etc.	Every 3 months	COLP
Theft of client, personal or confidential data from office by third party	Procedure now in place for logging visitors and supervising on site	Every 3 months	COLP
Client, personal or confidential data belonging to firm found in a skip or landfill	Ensure hard copy client, personal or confidential data is disposed via shredder or verified confidential waste	Every 6 months	COLP
Client, personal or confidential data belonging to firm found on second-hand PC equipment outside office premises	At end of life cycle, hard drives and media should be wiped and destroyed as soon as practicable. Destruction certificates should be obtained for all devices if external contractors are used for destruction	Every 6 months	COLP
Loss of client, personal or confidential data through third-party supplier	Carry out due diligence on third-party data standards before terms agreed and carry out regular independent assessment of cyber security competence of supplier	Every 6 months	COLP
Firm taking payments via credit or debit card	Ensure firm adheres to Payment Card Industry Data Security Standards (PCI DSS)	Annually	COLP

Annex 6B

File audit – cyber security supplement

Note: Your firm should have a file audit system in place carried out using an established template. These questions are to be *added* to your *existing* file audit as a cyber security supplement. It is *not* intended to *replace* your existing file audit system in its entirety.

Client personal data and ID

1. Has any personal data (including ID, bank account information, details of assets, estates or property, photographic or video material, medical records or any other information that could identify clients) been sent via unencrypted or unsecure means to clients or any other third party?

☐ (A) Yes ☐ (B) No

If you answered (A) Yes:

What data was sent and why did this happen?

____

☐ Tick to confirm fee earner has been advised and is aware of an action in breach of firm cyber security policy

☐ Tick to confirm the COLP has been notified

2. Have all clients been advised on the risks of sending personal data (including ID), commercially sensitive or confidential data via unencrypted email or other means to the firm?

☐ (A) Yes ☐ (B) No

If you answered (B) No, state why not:

____

3. Is there evidence on file that fee earners have double-checked receipt of any instructions from clients, financial institutions or any other third party regarding the use of client monetary funds or assets?

☐ (A) Yes ☐ (B) No

If you answered (B) No, state why not:

____

4. Is there evidence on file that any personal data, commercially sensitive data or confidential data sent via USB, CD-ROM or DVD-ROM was encrypted with appropriate encryption keys in accordance with the firm's cyber security policy?

☐ (A) Yes ☐ (B) No

If you answered (B) No, state why not:

____

5. Is there evidence on file that recipients of any encrypted data from this firm received the encryption key via appropriate means to enable data to be accessed?

☐ (A) Yes ☐ (B) No

If you answered (B) No, state why not:

____

Counsel

6. Have all counsel been advised on the risks of sending personal data, commercially sensitive or confidential data via unencrypted email to the firm?

☐ (A) Yes ☐ (B) No ☐ (C) N/A

If you answered (B) No, state why not:

____

Experts

7. Have all experts been advised on the risks of sending personal data, commercially sensitive or confidential data via unencrypted email to the firm?

☐ (A) Yes ☐ (B) No ☐ (C) N/A

If you answered (B) No, state why not:

____

8. Have all other solicitors/lawyers been advised on the risks of sending personal data, commercially sensitive or confidential data via unencrypted email to the firm?

☐ (A) Yes ☐ (B) No ☐ (C) N/A

If you answered (B) No, state why not:

____

9. Have all witnesses been advised on the risks of sending personal data, commercially sensitive or confidential data via unencrypted email to the firm?

☐ (A) Yes ☐ (B) No ☐ (C) N/A

If you answered (B) No, state why not:

____

10. Have all banks/financial institutions been advised on the risks of sending personal data, commercially sensitive or confidential data via unencrypted email to the firm?

☐ (A) Yes ☐ (B) No ☐ (C) N/A

If you answered (B) No, state why not:

____

11. Have all other third parties been advised on the risks of sending personal data, commercially sensitive or confidential data via unencrypted email to the firm?

☐ (A) Yes ☐ (B) No

If you answered (B) No, state why not:

____

Annex 6C

COLP cyber security action list

Governance

- Cyber security policy containing all cyber security procedures in place.
- Cyber security breach reporting mechanism in place for all staff.
- Plan in place to deal with a cyber security breach.
- Social media use policy in place for all staff, covering use of business social media and also social media in a personal capacity.
- Policies in place to ensure member(s) of staff responsible for cyber security report directly to and support COLP.
- Bring your own device (BYOD) policy in place if BYOD permitted.

Training and assessment

- Induction cyber security training for all new starters.
- All new starters to pass induction cyber security assessment with pass/fail mark.
- Cyber security refresher and update training for *all* staff every six months.
- Key staff to undertake cyber security breach simulation every six months.

Recruitment

- Occupational reference checks carried out on all new staff.
- Academic reference checks carried out on all new staff.
- Criminal record checks carried out on all new staff.
- 'New staff' is taken to include contractors, consultants or anyone else with regular access to the workplace.

Data access privileges

- Access to the system must be tailored to each role in the firm, with access only given for purposes necessary for fulfilling each role.
- Unique accounts for each user, including each administrator user.
- Controls put in place governing each administrator profile and its user.
- Password policy adhered to throughout the firm.
- Regular reviews of client, financial and HR data carried out to check for unauthorised access, abuse or anomalies.
- System put in place for storing client ID, client documents and client financial details, using suitable security, encryption and obscured details where necessary.

Controls – monitoring access to client data

- System put in place to restrict access to customer data and provide verification that client data has only been accessed, copied or downloaded for specified tasks.

Controls – data transmission

- All personal data sent by firm must be encrypted, whether it is sent by email or other online methods.

System security controls

- Regular penetration testing in place for all IT systems.
- IT systems are patched to protect against vulnerabilities.
- IT systems have most recent versions of antivirus software fitted, with updates enabled.
- Firewall(s) are in place, with updates enabled.
- The firm's external facing IP addresses are subject to regular vulnerability tests [*describe testing regime*].
- Regular assessments in place to monitor the sending of confidential or personal data as attachments via email.

Software controls

- All data-processing software in use has been built by software developers trained in the secure development of software.
- All data-processing software has been developed against a secure software development standard.

Back-up controls

- Assessments carried out to monitor end-to-end risks from back-up process.
- Secure encrypted links used for data transfer if backup carried out online.
- Offsite back-up is encrypted.
- Partial and full restore from backup is regularly tested to ensure integrity of backup.

Desktop controls

- Application put in place to detect loss of or access to client/personal data via email, portable media, social media and any other data channels.
- All antivirus programs or firewalls used to detect intrusion/penetration are active and up to date.

Mobile device control (including laptops)

- All devices are encrypted.
- Register of all devices issued to staff is maintained.
- Devices are regularly audited to ensure client/personal data is only accessible to those authorised to use it and to ensure that each staff member has access for a necessary, genuine business reason.
- If staff are permitted to undertake work from their own devices, appropriate security measures and checks must be used; otherwise, BYOD must not be permitted.

Portable media controls (including USB flash drives, CD-ROMs, DVD-ROMs, etc.)

- Only those with genuine business need are authorised to remove personal data to portable media. Regularly review staff members who have been granted authorisation to ensure integrity is maintained.
- Staff must ensure any client/personal data removed to portable media is securely encrypted.
- Regularly review the copying client/personal data to portable media to confirm there is always a genuine business need for it.

Data residency

- Data must be held in the UK or in a state covered by the GDPR or EU-US Privacy Shield [*state location of data*].

Office security measures

- Access to areas storing client/personal data (including server rooms, call centres, filing cabinets, etc.) is securely controlled [*state measures in place (e.g. fob, keypad, etc.)*].
- Procedure put in place for logging visitors and supervising on site.
- Procedure put in place for safe disposal of client/personal data (e.g. shredder, confidential waste bin, etc.).
- Procedure put in place for prompt, secure destruction of defunct hard drives and media.
- Destruction certificates must be obtained for all devices if external contractors are used for destruction.

Firm third-party suppliers

- Carry out due diligence on third-party data standards before terms are agreed.
- Perform regular audits of any third party's cyber security systems.
- Third-party suppliers must be required to report cyber security breaches within set time limits.

Payment Card Industry Data Security Standard

> **Note:** The Payment Card Industry Data Security Standard (PCI DSS) is a international standard established to ensure the secure processing of card payments and to help businesses reduce card fraud. See **www.theukcardsassociation.org.uk/security/what_is_PCI DSS.asp** for more information.

- Ensure the firm is PCI DSS compliant if the firm takes card payments.

Annex 6D

Periodic review – cyber security supplement

> **Note:** Your firm should have a periodic review system in place carried out using an established template. These questions are to be added to your existing periodic review as a cyber security supplement. It is not intended to replace your existing periodic review system in its entirety.

Cyber security governance

1. Is your firm's cyber security policy up to date?

☐ (A) Yes ☐ (B) No

If you answered (B) No, what action is being taken to bring it fully up to date?

____

2. Is your firm's breach reporting structure document up to date with the correct staff named and all responsibilities detailed?

☐ (A) Yes ☐ (B) No

If you answered (B) No, provide details of when reporting structure will be updated:

____

3. Are the cyber security sections of your firm's risk register up to date?

☐ (A) Yes ☐ (B) No

If you answered (B) No, provide details of when the cyber security sections of the risk register will be updated:

____

Cyber security breach reporting

4. List any cyber security breaches sustained by the firm in the last review period:

____

5. Has the firm's professional indemnity insurer been notified of the cyber security breach(es)?

☐ (A) Yes ☐ (B) No ☐ (C) N/A

If you answered (A) Yes, what was the outcome with the firm's professional indemnity insurer?

____

If you answered (B) No, why has the firm's professional indemnity insurer not been notified of the cyber security breach(es)?

____

6. Has the firm's cyber security insurer been notified of the cyber security breach(es)?

☐ (A) Yes ☐ (B) No ☐ (C) N/A

If you answered (A) Yes, what was the outcome with the cyber insurer?

____

If you answered (B) No, why has the cyber insurer not been notified of the cyber security breach(es)?

____

7. Has the SRA been notified of the cyber security breach(es)?

☐ (A) Yes ☐ (B) No ☐ (C) N/A

If you answered (A) Yes, what was the outcome with the SRA?

____

If you answered (B) No, why has the SRA not been notified of the cyber security breach(es)?

____

8. Has the ICO been notified of the cyber security breach(es)?

☐ (A) Yes ☐ (B) No ☐ (C) N/A

If you answered (A) Yes, what was the outcome with the ICO?

____

If you answered (B) No, why has the ICO not been notified of the cyber security breach(es)?

____

9. Have the police been notified of the cyber security breach(es)?

☐ (A) Yes ☐ (B) No ☐ (C) N/A

If you answered (A) Yes, what was the outcome with the police?

____

If you answered (B) No, why have the police not been notified of the cyber security breach(es)?

____

10. Have the affected clients been notified of the cyber security breach(es)?

☐ (A) Yes ☐ (B) No ☐ (C) N/A

If you answered (B) No, why have the affected clients not been notified of the cyber security breach(es)?

____

11. Have all staff members been informed of the nature and consequences of the cyber security breach(es)?

☐ (A) Yes ☐ (B) No ☐ (C) N/A

If you answered (B) No, why have the staff not been notified of the nature and consequences of the cyber security breach(es)?

____

12. If the cyber security breach(es) involved staff personal data, have all affected staff members been informed?

☐ (A) Yes ☐ (B) No ☐ (C) N/A

If you answered (B) No, why have the staff not been notified of the cyber security breach(es)?

____

13. Has the firm's bank been informed of the cyber security breach(es)?

☐ (A) Yes ☐ (B) No ☐ (C) N/A

If you answered (B) No, why has the firm's bank not been notified of the cyber security breach(es)?

____

14. Have the client bank(s) or lender(s) been informed of the cyber security breach(es) involving clients' personal data?

☐ (A) Yes ☐ (B) No ☐ (C) N/A

If you answered (B) No, why have the client bank(s) or lender(s) not been informed of the cyber security breach(es) involving clients' personal data?

____

15. Have any client complaints been received as a result of the cyber security breach(es)?

☐ (A) Yes ☐ (B) No ☐ (C) N/A

If you answered (A) Yes, list the actions taken in response to the client complaints received as a result of cyber security breach(es):

____

16. Have any clients been lost as a result of the cyber security breach(es)?

☐ (A) Yes ☐ (B) No ☐ (C) N/A

If you answered (A) Yes, list the actions taken in response to having lost clients as a result of the cyber security breach(es):

____

17. Have all affected third parties/suppliers/contractors been notified as a result of cyber security breach(es) involving third parties'/suppliers'/contractors' systems or commercially sensitive data?

☐ (A) Yes ☐ (B) No ☐ (C) N/A

If you answered (B) No, why were third parties/suppliers/contractors not notified?

____

Cyber security file auditing

18. Is the firm's cyber security file auditing up to date during the review period?

☐ (A) Yes ☐ (B) No

If you answered (B) No, why is the cyber security element of the file auditing system not up to date during this review period?

____

19. Are the cyber security file auditing forms reviewed and up to date (reflecting best practice)?

☐ (A) Yes ☐ (B) No

If you answered (B) No, why are the cyber security file auditing forms not reviewed and up to date during this review period?

____

20. Is the cyber security file audit process working?

☐ (A) Yes ☐ (B) No

If you answered (B) No, what action is being taken to ensure that the cyber security file audit process is improved and works properly and effectively for the firm?

____

21. Have any negative patterns been identified as a result of the cyber security audit process?

☐ (A) Yes ☐ (B) No

If you answered (A) Yes, what action is being taken to analyse the reasons for these patterns and to take corrective measures?

____

22. Have any required corrective actions been identified from the cyber security file auditing?

☐ (A) Yes ☐ (B) No

If you answered (A) Yes, list the corrective actions and detail the roadmap to carry out the corrective actions necessary:

____

Staff, support and training

23. Is there a cyber security officer (CSO) in place to support the COLP?

☐ (A) Yes ☐ (B) No

If you answered (B) No, why is the COLP handling the cyber security threat to the firm on his/her own with no support?

____

24. Is there a cyber security working group in place to support the CSO and COLP? [May not be applicable for sole practitioner or small firms.]

☐ (A) Yes ☐ (B) No

If you answered (B) No, why is there no wider working group in place to support the cyber security compliance work of the CSO and COLP?

____

25. Have the CSO and COLP attended advanced external cyber security training in the last 12 months, for dissemination across firm?

☐ (A) Yes ☐ (B) No

If you answered (B) No, what steps are being taken to ensure the COLP, CSO and firm remain up to date on current advanced cyber security threats to businesses, the legal profession and the firm in particular?

____

26. In the last six months, have all staff received either cyber security refresher training or (for new starters, up to and including new starters in the last 14 days) a cyber security induction?

☐ (A) Yes ☐ (B) No

If you answered (B) No, state when the inductions and refresher training sessions are scheduled to take place and list the reasons why this has not taken place during review period:

____

27. Have all staff (up to and including new starters in the last 14 days) passed the cyber security assessment with the correct pass level?

☐ (A) Yes ☐ (B) No

If you answered (B) No, state when the cyber security assessment is scheduled to take place and list reasons why this has not taken place during the review period:

____

28. Is the content of the staff cyber security training reviewed every six months?

☐ (A) Yes ☐ (B) No

If you answered (B) No, why has content of staff cyber security training not been reviewed for more than six months?

____

Firm website

29. Is the firm's website secure and up to date (including all apps, plug-ins, security certificates and domain registrations)?

☐ (A) Yes ☐ (B) No

If you answered (B) No, why is the website not secure and up to date?

____

30. State the date of the last meeting with the web developer to review security and threats to the website:

[*dd/mm/yyyy*]

If meeting was more than six months ago, please explain reason:

____

31. Is the website backed up in accordance with the firm's back-up policy?

☐ (A) Yes ☐ (B) No

If you answered (B) No, state why not:

____

Remote working

32. Is the register of staff with remote working privileges up to date?

☐ (A) Yes ☐ (B) No

If you answered (B) No, state why not:

____

33. Has the staff system access been reviewed, and any obsolete user profiles deleted?

☐ (A) Yes ☐ (B) No

If you answered (B) No, state why not:

____

Firm social media

33.	**Has the social media pledge been signed by all staff?**
	☐ (A) Yes ☐ (B) No
	If you answered (B) No, state why not:
	____

Passwords

35.	**Have random checks on staff been performed to ensure password policy is being adhered to?**
	☐ (A) Yes ☐ (B) No
	If you answered (B) No, state why not:
	____

Annex 6E

IT security checklist – quick questions

> **Note:** Ask your firm's IT department to record these answers so you have a concise, accessible summary of your cyber security status to give the SRA in the event of a cyber security breach (**N.B.** These quick questions are not intended to replace the more comprehensive questionnaire at **Annex 2A**).
>
> This checklist may also be useful if you need a brief overview of a potential supplier's cyber security strength. (**N.B.** These quick questions are not intended to replace the more comprehensive questionnaire at **Annex 8A**).

- Is your firm's server (whether a physical or cloud-based server) encrypted?
- Is your firm's email encrypted?
    - If not, how should personal data be safely transmitted into and out of your firm?
- Does your firm use a virtual private network (VPN)?
- Does your firm use anti-malware software?
    - If so, how often is a scan performed?
- Does your firm provide mobile devices for staff?
    - If so, are they encrypted?
- How often do you assess and evaluate your firm's IT security?

7 Staff training

7.1 The need for training

Any review of office best practice should begin with staff and their training and education. In the instance of cyber security, training on best practice should focus on creating a general awareness of risks and emphasising the importance of internal governance measures. Cyber security requires top-to-bottom training – picking up staff when they first join while also regularly updating existing staff on any significant developments or changes. Training should be delivered to all levels of the business, from the most junior paralegals, trainees and administrators all the way through to partners, heads of departments and senior management.

7.2 Governance of training methods

Training methods and materials needs to be backed up by supporting documentation, e.g.: relevant policies, procedures, templates and checklists that are utilised and updated regularly. They cannot be allowed to gather dust on a shelf somewhere; they need to be handy, accessible documents that staff are encouraged to regularly refer to.

Staff should also be encouraged to actively engage with the policies and procedures – to give feedback on what works and what doesn't, what is no longer relevant and what new risks need to be added. If staff find new rules or procedures restrictive, see if they can be modified. If staff and fee earners are taking steps to circumvent any cyber security measures, find out why. Is the reason due to the complexity of what is being asked? Is one particular procedure too time-consuming, prompting staff to take a time-saving shortcut instead? Or has a client given negative feedback? Whatever the reason, listen to the feedback, understand why a measure is not working, and modify it until it is acceptable to staff, management and clients – but still achieves the appropriate level of cyber security.

7.3 Delivering training

7.3.1 Engaging training methods

Training must be engaging and interesting; sessions based around a speaker reading endless slides will not be effective. A monotonous lecture will probably achieve nothing except a room full of staff looking at their watches or gazing into space. It is essential that the training methods encourage staff to properly think about the information and how it applies to their day-to-day roles.

An effective training session must:

- start with a clear explanation of why the training is happening and what the desired outcomes are;
- be broken down into concise points (avoiding jargon where possible) supported by practical demonstrations and interactive tasks; and
- have plenty of opportunities to ask questions and give feedback.

The precise format of training will depend on the firm's size and character. It is likely that your firm already uses a trusted training provider, one with a proven record of achieving results with your staff. Identify what it is that is effective in their training – format, presentation style, use of technology, interactivity, etc. – and look to secure a suitable cyber security training provider with similar strengths.

7.3.2 Who to train, and when

Cyber security training for all staff

All staff, no matter their level of seniority, need to receive training. You must ensure that everyone – from the person opening the post to the senior partner – is aware of cyber security threats and how to combat them.

Due to time pressures and a perceived lack of relevance, senior management in many firms will skip any training sessions, thinking that something else is more important, that a handout can be read afterwards instead or that it applies more to other staff and not to them. This is not acceptable. In April 2016, when the Law Society Gazette reported that 48 top law firms had been hacked for mergers and acquisition information ('M&A hack attack on 48 elite law firms', Chloe Smith, *Law Society Gazette*, 4 April 2016, pp.1–2), the cyber director at insurance broker Willis FINEX Global remarked that one of the common problems was that the hackers were often able to easily access cloud-based Dropbox accounts used by senior partners – who were using the system in direct contravention of their own firm's information security policies.

It is of fundamental importance that all staff – all pay grades and all partners or directors – attend and fully understand any sessions that introduce cyber security governance measures or threat updates. They cannot be allowed to become the weak link in a firm's defences against fraud and cyber attacks. A lack of awareness of these issues at any level of an organisation will open up the weaknesses that training was supposed to address in the first place. The closest thing that your firm has to a three-line whip should be enforced to ensure attendance at training sessions and follow-up assessments. There have been instances where chief executives themselves have been responsible for a cyber security breach, due to a lack of awareness of their own security measures. You don't want the same thing to happen at your firm.

Induction training

Provide induction training for new starters within one week of starting employment at the organisation. The risk from external cyber threats is too great to exacerbate that risk by allowing new starters to access the firm's networks, confidential data or email system without suitable cyber security awareness. Delaying induction training could make the firm vulnerable to attacks such as phishing emails or targeted fraud.

Regardless of how junior or senior they may be, or the training and knowledge they may have previously acquired, staff must be quickly and efficiently brought up to speed on the type of cyber security threats that your organisation will face and the specific technical and governance measures in place to combat them.

Refresher training

Cyber security threats evolve and change all the time, so refresher training for *all* staff (including partners, senior managers, etc.) should take place at least every six months. It should be interactive, offer staff a chance to be consulted on new measures before they are introduced, and build a more inclusive and collaborative environment where all staff are engaged in protecting the firm and its clients.

It is important that your staff are kept up to date with news of any recent attacks in other organisations. This information will remind staff that cyber attacks are a risk to be taken seriously, and also help them learn from the mistakes of others.

Any measures taken by your firm – whether a new question on the regular internal file audit form or a check applied to all individuals calling the office to discuss financial issues – should be properly explained to your staff. Staff are more likely to conscientiously follow measures if they understand the reasoning behind them and why they have to be taken. Also, staff members may have valuable input on how steps can be made more effective.

7.4 Staff assessment

Training should be backed up by suitably rigorous assessment. Having a form of practical assessment ensures that the key messages from the training session have been assimilated by the staff, helps them retain the information, and also provides management with a clear, measurable result.

The assessment might be carried out on the day of the training, or afterwards. It does not have to be a heavy-duty exam with endless questions and strict pass/fail criteria. It could be a list of 15 multiple-choice questions that pick up on the themes discussed in the training session. The questions should be based on practical issues that could arise during the day-to-day operation of the business. This will encourage staff to think about the impact of the cyber security measures and how the procedures will fit in with their everyday work.

If your firm has the resources, providing the assessment as an online format has many benefits. It makes it easier to regularly change the questions and will also allow for assessment records to be maintained for each member of staff, ensuring that each employee has fully up-to-date records that can be reviewed easily by management.

Whatever format the assessment takes, the results should be monitored and anyone scoring less than 80% should be quietly asked to undertake a second assessment to ensure understanding and compliance with the firm's cyber security governance. Setting a pass mark of around 80% will make it easy to see whether staff have understood the risks and the safeguards that your organisation is trying to take.

Annex 7A

Staff training checklist

- Train staff according to the key risks identified by your firm; e.g. if you hold client money make sure staff are trained in the particular risks involving banking, email and money transfers.
- Have policies and training about email and telephone usage as well as use of personal and mobile devices.
- Have clear and up-to-date policies in place for dealing with scams, and ensure the policies cover the risk from insider activity.
- Training should be an ongoing activity to reflect the rate at which new cyber risks emerge.

The following is a non-exclusive list of topics that must be included in any regular cyber security staff training course:

- Password security and periodic password change
- Email security (including encryption and transmission of personal data, and two-factor authentication
- How to spot phishing emails
- Risks of remote working [including the risks from insecure public and home WiFi networks]
- Mobile device use
- Awareness of legal and regulatory requirements
- Software and other tools to avoid cyber security breaches
- Examples of relevant cyber security breaches
- Examples of recent (within the last 3–6 months) cyber attacks
- Examples of social manipulation [e.g. client/third-party impersonation via email, fraudulent phone calls to elicit transfer details, etc.]
- Examples of social media exploitation
- Examples of environmental manipulation risks (e.g. the risk that a public power socket will have been tampered with so it transfers malware onto any mobile device plugged into it (this is known as 'juice jacking'))
- Data storage and data retention procedures
- Bring your own device (BYOD) best practice, if firm permits BYOD
- Potential future threats
- Regulatory changes anticipated in next few years

Annex 7B

Individual cyber security training log

Name:

Frequency of training: [e.g. 6 months]

Date	Title of training	Type of training	Trainer	Competency [Y/N]	Notes

Annex 7C

Staff survey – cyber security risk assessment

1. Have you ever received training in data protection while working at this business?

☐ (A) Yes ☐ (B) No ☐ (C) Don't know

2. Have you ever heard of the Data Protection Act 1998 during your time with this business?

☐ (A) Yes ☐ (B) No ☐ (C) Don't know

3. Have you seen your business's employee handbook and are you familiar with its contents?

☐ (A) Yes ☐ (B) No ☐ (C) Don't know

4. Have you read your business's data protection policy?

☐ (A) Yes ☐ (B) No ☐ (C) Don't know

5. Have you ever used Dropbox or other freely available cloud-based solutions such as Google Drive to share business documents?

☐ (A) Yes ☐ (B) No ☐ (C) Don't know

6. Have you ever used a USB drive to store or transfer business documents?

☐ (A) Yes ☐ (B) No ☐ (C) Don't know

7. How does your office send personal data to other branch offices?

____

8. How does your business share documents with partner organisations or clients?

☐ (A) Email ☐ (B) Data room

☐ (C) Shared server ☐ (D) Post

☐ (E) Other

Please state: ________________________________

9. Does your business use Hotmail/Gmail or other web-based email for business correspondence?

☐ (A) Yes ☐ (B) No ☐ (C) Don't know

10. Does your business send personal data via email? (Personal data is defined as anything that allows you to identify an individual, e.g. names, addresses, dates of birth, ID, photos, video, audio recordings, etc.)

☐ (A) Yes ☐ (B) No ☐ (C) Don't know

11. Does your business have a disaster recovery plan?

☐ (A) Yes ☐ (B) No *Please go to Question 12.* ☐ (C) Don't know *Please go to Question 12.*

If you answered (A) Yes, where is the disaster recovery plan kept and who is responsible for it?

____

12. In the event you could not access your office for a day, are you aware how you would access your phones and data and be able to work away from the office?

____

13. Does your business use video conferencing?

☐ (A) Yes ☐ (B) No *Please go to Question 14.* ☐ (C) Don't know *Please go to Question 14.*

If you answered (A) Yes, please state the name of your video conference provider.

____

14. Does your business use Skype to make calls or communicate using instant messaging?

☐ (A) Yes ☐ (B) No *Please go to Question 15.* ☐ (C) Don't know *Please go to Question 15.*

If you answered (A) Yes, what is Skype used for?

☐ (i) Internal staff communications only (e.g. inter-office or remote working)

☐ (iii) External communication with clients

☐ (ii) External communication with third-party contractors

☐ (iv) Other

Please state:

____

15. Does your business send personal data by Royal Mail post?

☐ (A) Yes ☐ (B) No *Please go to Question 16.* ☐ (C) Don't know *Please go to Question 16.*

If you answered (A) Yes, what class of post?

☐ (i) First class ☐ (iii) Other *Please state*: ____________

☐ (ii) Second class

AND How does the post leave the office?

☐ (i) Collected by Royal Mail staff ☐ (iii) Other *Please state*: ____________

☐ (ii) Taken to post office/box by member of staff ☐ (iv) Don't know

16. Does your business use Royal Mail special delivery for any items?

☐ (A) Yes ☐ (B) No ☐ (C) Don't know

17. Does your business ever use a third-party courier?

☐ (A) Yes ☐ (B) No ☐ (C) Don't know

18. Does your business have a fax machine?

☐ (A) Yes ☐ (B) No *Please go to Question 19.* ☐ (C) Don't know *Please go to Question 19.*

If you answered (A) Yes, how many staff share the use of each fax machine?

____

19. Does your business provide staff with IT equipment (including mobile devices such as smartphones, tablet PCs, laptops, etc.)?

☐ (A) Yes ☐ (B) No ☐ (C) Don't know

20. Does your business allow staff to carry out work duties on their own mobile devices and IT hardware (including desktops, laptops, tablets, smartphones, etc.)?

☐ (A) Yes ☐ (B) No ☐ (C) Don't know

21. Does your business require staff to regularly change their passwords? (This includes passwords for any case management system, document management system, client relationship management system, accounts package, IT hardware and any corporate social media accounts.)

☐ (A) Yes ☐ (B) No ☐ (C) Don't know

22. Do the staff members wear ID/lanyards?

☐ (A) Yes ☐ (B) No *Please go to Question 23.* ☐ (C) Don't know *Please go to Question 23.*

If you answered (A) Yes, who is responsible for distributing ID/lanyards and for collecting them when staff leave the business?

____

23. Do you have a clear-desk policy at your office?

☐ (A) Yes ☐ (B) No ☐ (C) Don't know

24. Any additional comments?

____

8 Cyber security solutions – technology

Cyber security governance can be split into two broad categories:

- **personnel**: advising staff how they *should* act to ensure data protection (see **Chapter 9**); and
- **technology**: using defensive IT systems to protect, and restrict access to, company networks – so that certain actions *won't* threaten data protection (the subject of this chapter).

While there will inevitably be some overlap between the two categories, it is helpful to make this division when first getting to grips with the complexities of cyber security governance – especially when deciding how to allocate time and resources most effectively.

8.1 Ensuring technology is defensive

Maintaining suitable defence levels across all IT platforms is a matter of both initial investment (whether that is merely the time and effort of researching the best low-cost solution, or paying for a premium service) and continual monitoring and maintenance.

General security measures begin with a firewall around the system to prevent unauthorised access and activity. Regular updating of operating systems and internet browsers is necessary to ensure they remain resistant to the ever-changing range of cyber security threats.

> *Action point – Updating IT policies*
>
> Continually update your firm's IT best practice policy with information on current risks and best practice. Provide regular refresher training to staff; do not leave them to combat today's sophisticated threats with outdated knowledge half-remembered from a course three years ago.

8.1.1 Network security

IT systems and networks are literally where most legal work happens now. Having that network compromised, weakened or at worst taken down completely is a huge risk. Focusing on understanding and implementing network security is as important as staff training but is in some ways more daunting. This section covers what network security entails and how to decide the best way to secure your specific network.

A robust network security system should:

- protect your networks against external and internal attack;
- manage the network perimeter;
- filter out unauthorised access and malicious content;
- have the capability to set network permissions which limit what files can be downloaded and saved onto the network;
- monitor and test security controls;
- include malware protection;
- have anti-malware defences that are applicable and relevant to all business areas; and
- scan for malware across the organisation.

Premium antivirus software is available, but if you are working to a tight budget, there are low-cost or free solutions available. Comodo (**www.comodo.com**) is a free antivirus package that includes firewall protection. It will screen any WiFi network a laptop is about to connect to, as well as screening anything that is downloaded. It can also be used on mobile devices.

Malware can be scanned using premium software but a free solution called Malwarebytes (**www.malwarebytes.com**) is available. Once downloaded to a device it will conduct a scan of all files and identify any corrupt or suspicious files.

For the majority of users, limit the system access so staff members cannot download program or apps that could contain malware.

> *Action point – Monitoring software*
>
> Regularly carry out a physical check on all devices for any poor performance, recurring 'pop up' ads that were not requested or other signs that could indicate the presence of malware.

8.1.2 Secure configuration

The default installation settings on computers and network devices are not necessarily secure and can provide cyber criminals with opportunities to gain access to sensitive information, often quite easily. Applying simple security controls can minimise inherent weaknesses and increase your protection. Strong, secure configuration can include:

- Application of security patches and maintaining the secure configuration of all IT systems.
- Having a system inventory and baseline specification for all IT systems.
- Ensuring your system is up to date (for example, Windows withdrew support for Windows XP in 2014 and the platform is not secure).
- Enabling the platform feature that ensures active updates are taking place.
- Ensuring all versions of Internet Explorer, Firefox, Chrome or any other browser commonly used are fully up to date, with relevant security.
- The removal or disabling of unnecessary software.
- Enabling personal firewalls on desktop PCs and laptops so that they are configured to block unapproved connections by default.

Action point – Further solutions

The following external providers can help with encryption, malware and BYOD office solutions.

Free:

- 7-Zip (encryption of attachments to email) – **www.7-zip.org**
- Malwarebytes (malware scanning and removal) – **www.malwarebytes.com.**
- Comodo (firewall and antivirus provider) – **www.comodo.com.**

Low cost:

- The Link App (secure client communication via a mobile app) – **www.thelinkapp.co.uk.**
- GCI (secure remote mobile desktop) – **www.gcicom.net.**
- Fitzrovia IT (secure BYOD access to business email and apps) – **www.fitzroviait.com.**

The government's Cyber Essentials Scheme is a useful source of further guidance on basic cyber security requirements within businesses. See **www.gov.uk/government/publications/cyber-essentials-scheme-overview** for more information.

8.1.3 Legacy IT systems

Firms need to ensure that their operating systems function securely both at present and in the future. Many law firms made a substantial initial investment in IT in the late 1990s and early 2000s, and these older systems may now be using old, unsupported versions of Windows or Internet Explorer. If such products are unsupported, the developer, in this case Microsoft, is no longer supplying updates and patches to deal with any possible cyber security weaknesses.

For example, one of Microsoft's most popular operating systems was Windows XP, and after 12 years of development, support for the system ceased in 2014. However, many business users continue to use the system, along with obsolete versions of Internet Explorer, leaving themselves vulnerable to exploitation.

The same risks are present with any online systems that your firm could be using – from email to case management or communication – and regular checks should be carried out to ensure that all of the systems your firm relies on continue to operate in a secure and up-to-date manner.

8.1.4 Using cloud services

Due to the high levels of client confidentiality required by law firms, you should always conduct due diligence on any proposed third-party provider to ensure that they can meet the requirements of a legal business before they make a final commitment.

According to the SRA, best practice for due diligence includes:

- taking references from other companies that have used the proposed provider;
- checking service level agreements carefully to ensure that the proposed service will be compliant with the EU-US Privacy Shield if data is stored outside the European Economic Area (EEA);
- checking that the provider can offer audited information security that, at a minimum, is compliant with ISO/IEC 27001:2013;
- checking that the provider can offer a level of guaranteed uptime and continuity protection that is acceptable to the firm;
- ensuring, if staff will be working remotely, that they have properly secured communication channels to protect security; and
- ensuring that the contract with the provider includes the requirements of outcome 7.10 of the SRA Code of Conduct 2011.

Security can also be improved by:

- using a private cloud, or private area of a hybrid cloud, for client confidential material;
- using software to automatically encrypt documents at the law firm's end, using security keys that are not known to the provider; and
- using only providers based in EEA countries (or countries offering equivalent or greater data protection laws) who can guarantee that data will not be held in jurisdictions that do not offer such protections.

8.1.5 Electronic back-up/recovery

A formal back-up system is required to ensure business continuity of the firm if there is any loss of data or corruption of data within the firm's IT systems. This back-up needs to be robust enough to ensure that the business can continue to function safely, no loss of data, after a cyber attack or system failure, but also after a wider infrastructure failure, such as the loss of power or loss of access to one, or all, of the firm's physical offices.

This should ensure that the firm can still function in the event of a cyber attack, major power cut or major incident (including manmade or natural disasters) near any of its offices.

A back-up system should include two distinct and separate locations where data will be backed-up to. Plans should also be in place for the phones to be diverted and there should be a system for notifying staff in the event that they are unable to access their place of work.

Any back-up system should be rigorously tested to ensure that a full system reset and restore is possible, and also that individual files or records can be restored in isolation. The full disaster and recovery back-up system should be tested every three months to check that data is being correctly backed-up; regular testing is essential, otherwise any flaws in the back-up system will only be discovered after a failure of the day-to-day system, by which time it would be too late and data will have been lost.

8.1.6 Technology/data destruction

Every firm must have a clear policy for destroying obsolete IT hardware. If this is handled by the firm's IT supplier, a destruction certificate must be obtained from the supplier, for *every* piece of equipment they destroy that contains a hard drive. Under no circumstances should the firm accept just one certificate to cover a batch of devices.

If a third-party contractor is appointed to handle the destruction of the firm's IT hardware, they should be assessed to confirm that:

- they will provide individual destruction certificates for all hardware;
- they will either destroy equipment onsite or provide audio-visual confirmation of the destruction of hardware; and
- they have previous experience in destroying IT hardware for other well-known professional services firms.

Any third-party contractor should be accompanied at all times by firm staff while onsite at the firm. Contractors should not be unaccompanied at any time while on the firm's premises (including front of house or back office locations).

8.2 Access restrictions

The consequences of having a system that is open to access abuse are severe. In the case of Mossack Fonseca, a member of staff was able to access a broad range of files from across many departments, including archived files. On their website the firm stated proudly that their IT was 'secure, state of the art technology... upgraded continually'. The fact that they were hacked and a significant amount of documents leaked clearly shows that the firm's IT was not as secure as they thought.

8.2.1 Managing user privileges

User accounts with special access privileges typically have the greatest access to key information. When privileged accounts are compromised it can result in extensive corruption of information. To protect against user access abuse:

- Establish account management processes and limit the number of privileged accounts.
- Limit user privileges and monitor user activity.
- Limit system access so staff only have access to the files and directories that they need to carry out their roles. Do all staff need access to all client matters? Do all staff need access to old archived files?
- Have tracking systems in place so it is possible to identify who accessed which files, who downloaded any documents or files, and where they were downloaded to. This information is available on all systems but often only revealed after an expensive forensic examination of a hard drive or server; however, it can be accessed routinely for management administration purposes on some systems.
- Control access to activity and audit logs.
- Limit how data can be removed from a system. Lock off the use of USB ports to prevent the unauthorised removal of any files from the system. Also block access to file transfer sites like Dropbox or Google Docs. Block access to webmail accounts like Gmail or Yahoo. If staff need to access personal email they can do it from their own devices in their own time. The risk of sensitive files being removed from the business networks via personal email is simply too great.

8.2.2 Home and mobile working

Although the flexibility of home and mobile working offers many benefits to businesses, the cyber risks must not be underestimated. It is better to restrict remote working and maintain high levels of security than encourage flexible working practices when the firm does not have the systems in place to ensure such methods are secure.

Appropriate systems to have in place include:

- developing a remote working policy and training staff to adhere to it (see **Annex 9E**);
- applying the secure baseline build to all authorised mobile devices;
- protecting data both in transit and at rest;
- adopting an end-to-end solution so that data remains safe and secure no matter where it is being accessed from.

The remote working policy should be tailored to suit the firm's specific business needs; key points worth considering are:

- Will the policy permit users to carry out work-related activity on their own personal devices or on devices provided by the business?
- What security will be mandated to be in place on all devices? What encryption and security levels? What antivirus software?
- Some IT providers now provide secure access to business related apps via personal devices – identify a suitable system and ensure it is used across the business at all levels regardless of seniority.

See **9.2.1–9.2.2** and **Annex 9A** for more details.

8.3 Staff and the use of technology

8.3.1 Training in IT systems

There's little point in investing in various cyber security IT systems if your staff do not know how to implement that technology properly. It is therefore important to promote proper use of the IT security solutions by:

- producing user policies covering acceptable and secure use of the organisation's systems;
- establishing a staff training programme;
- maintaining user awareness of cyber risks;
- ensuring governance is supported by a practical working structure and proactive attitude towards the necessary procedures (see **8.3.2**); and
- providing effective training and assessment in cyber security risks and management for staff at all levels – regardless of seniority and mandated as part of induction process (see **Chapter** 7).

8.3.2 Responding to staff feedback

While network security measures can seem restrictive, it is crucial to ensure that they are not so restrictive that staff go to lengths to work around the very measures and systems that have been put in place to protect them and the organisation.

Procedures and systems may need to be tweaked and improved over time to take account for feedback from staff. Encourage everyone within the firm to take a proactive attitude towards the firm's security procedures and to voice their opinions. Staff feedback – on issues that could mean the systems are not working, not providing the security that they were intended to, or getting in the way of the smooth and effective running of the business – is key to maintaining effective, relevant and up-to-date cyber security.

Annex 8A

Cyber security compliance questionnaire for law firm suppliers/contractors

	Compliance requirement	Supplier response	Gap analysis	Risk assessment
	Governance procedures			
1	Cyber security risk has been acknowledged and is subject to specific policies, with a designated manager who has overall responsibility for risk assessment and management across the organisation. There is a clear mechanism for staff and partners to report cyber security breaches or issues.			
2	Clear action plan is in place to manage a cyber security breach or incident, including reporting mechanisms.			
	Training and assessment			
3	There is regular induction and refresher training on cyber security to staff, covering legal and regulatory requirements, best practice and possible consequences of a cyber security breach.			
4	Staff must undertake assessment with a certain pass grade following delivery of training.			
5	Regular training is delivered on remote-working practices (including travel, working in public locations and working at home).			

	Recruitment checks			
6	To control risk from fraud, background checks are carried out on all staff, including occupational history, criminal records, academic and vocational qualifications.			
	Data access privileges			
7	Access to the system is tailored to each role in the firm, with access only permitted for the purpose of fulfilling each role.			
8	Each user has a unique account, including each 'Administrator' user.			
9	Summarise any multiple additional 'Administrator' controls.			
10	There is a password policy in place requiring a minimum of 12-character passwords (including a number). Passwords must be regularly changed. [*If the password policy is weaker than described above, state reasons.*]			
11	User access is reviewed regularly for abuse and anomalies.			
12	Customer/client ID authentication details are stored using suitable security, encryption and obfuscation [*explain process in full.*]			
	Controls – customer data access monitoring			
13	Access system restricts access to customer data, and provides verification that it has not been accessed, copied or downloaded except for specific tasks.			

	Controls – data transmission			
14	Data is always encrypted during transmission, whether it is sent electronically or physically.			
	Controls – system security			
15	Regular penetration testing is carried out.			
16	IT systems are patched to protect against vulnerabilities.			
17	IT systems have most recent versions of antivirus software fitted, with updates enabled.			
18	Firewall(s) are in place and updates enabled.			
19	External facing IP addresses are subject to regular vulnerability tests [*describe testing regime*].			
20	Transmission of confidential or personal data via email is regularly assessed.			
	Controls – software			
21	All data-processing software in use has been built by software developers trained in the secure development of software.			
22	All data-processing software has been developed against a secure software development standard.			
	Controls – back-up			
23	End-to-end risks from back-up process are regularly assessed.			

24	Secure encrypted links are used for data transfer (if back-up carried out online). [*State to what standard.*]			
25	Physical offsite backup is encrypted. [*State to what standard.*]			
	Controls – desktop			
26	Application is in place to detect any loss of or access to data via email, portable media, social media or HTTP/S.			
27	Antivirus and firewalls are active and up to date to detect any intrusion/ penetration.			
	Controls – mobile devices (including laptops)			
28	All devices are encrypted.			
29	A full and accurate register of devices issued to staff is maintained.			
30	Devices are regularly audited to ensure customer data is only accessible to those authorised to use it and that it is properly necessary to have access, for a genuine business reason.			
	Controls – portable media (including USB flash drives, CD-ROMs, DVD-ROMs, etc.)			
31	Only those with genuine business need are authorised to remove customer data to portable media. This is reviewed regularly to ensure integrity.			

32	Staff are permitted to download customer data to portable media only so long as it is securely encrypted.			
33	A regular review is carried out of any copying of customer data to portable media to confirm genuine business need for it.			
34	All data on portable media is destroyed as soon as is reasonably practicable.			
	Data residency			
35	Data is held in the UK or in a state covered by the EU's General Data Protection Regulation or EU-US Privacy Shield [*confirm location of data*].			
	Office security measures			
36	There is controlled access to areas storing customer data (including server rooms, call centres, filing cabinets). [*State measures in place (e.g. fob, keypad etc.).*]			
37	List deterrents to fraudulent access (e.g. CCTV, grilles, alarms, security guards, etc.).			
38	There is a procedure in place for logging visitors and supervising onsite.			
	Disposal of customer data			
39	Customer data access is paperless where possible.			
40	Customer data is destroyed securely (e.g. shredder, confidential waste bin, etc.).			

41	Once out of use, hard drives and portable media are wiped and destroyed as soon as practicable.			
42	Destruction certificates are obtained for all devices from any external contractors used for destruction.			
43	All data belonging to customer as data controller or provided by customer or owned by customer under terms of contract securely returned at termination of relationship [*state method of transit and security measures used*].			
	Third-party suppliers			
44	Due diligence is carried out on third-party data standards before terms agreed.			
45	Third-party cyber security systems are regularly audited.			
46	Third-party suppliers are required to report cyber security breaches within set time limits.			
47	*No* third-party to access, copy, store or disclose data unless a term of the contract.			
	Payment Card Industry Data Security Standards (PCI DSS) compliance			
48	If payment card processing is taking place, PCI DSS compliance has been achieved. [*If non-compliant, state time frame to compliance and outstanding actions.*]			

49	State if the service provider agent is registered with the Visa Merchant Agent Registration scheme.			
50	Where an application integrates with a payment processor (e.g. Cybersource), the integration has been assessed and approved by a QSA.			

Contractor/supplier answers submitted on:	
Risk assessment of contractor answers completed on:	
Use of contractor permitted [Y/N]:	
Approved by COLP on:	

Annex 8B

Website management policy

1. Person with overall responsibility

   1.1 The person with overall responsibility for the [*name of practice*] website(s) is [*name and job title*]. In the event that [he/she] are absent or otherwise unavailable, queries should be addressed to [*name or function/job title and contact details*].

   1.2 [His/her] responsibilities include [*list of responsibilities and decision-making powers. You may also wish to exclude certain powers, for example, budget authorisation above a certain level. If so, how these decisions will be taken could be included in the policy*].

2. **Our website**

[*Set out the business objectives and plans for your website. A simple statement of the practice's objectives in relation to the site, how it will achieve them and how it plans to develop the site will help to clarify these matters and ensure that they are communicated throughout the practice. This section could include a general statement about the practice's approach to management of the site – a tight, centrally controlled approach or one which allows content owners more autonomy.*]

3. Website management

   3.1 Day-to-day operational control questions, including security matters, should be addressed to [*name or function/job title and contact details*].

   3.2 Other roles include [*list roles. If you have a large site with many different roles and responsibilities you may wish to set these out in a table along with contact details. Alternatively you may wish to simply put the principal contact in your policy and set out other roles and responsibilities in a separate document. This section should be distinguished from section 4 where key roles in relation to document approval and publishing should be identified.*]

4. Document approval and publishing

   4.1 Final responsibility for approving new or revised documents for publication on the website rests with [*name(s) and role(s)*].

   4.2 In this context 'document' includes [*list of types of publication that are subject to the approval and publication process*] and excludes [*for example, blogs, etc.*].

   4.3 Before publication is approved they [*or* you *if this is delegated to content owners*] will need to be satisfied that the document meets the required standards in the following areas:

      4.3.1 Compliance: [*set out standards of compliance and person responsible for sign-off*]

      4.3.2 Quality: [*set out standards of quality and person responsible for sign-off*]

4.3.3 Conformance: [*set out standards of conformance and person responsible for sign-off*]

4.4 They will also need to be satisfied that a review period or expiry date has been set.

5. Permitted and prohibited use

[*This section is most appropriate for setting out the limits of any delegated authority to update the content of the site, rather than regulatory compliance. How you intend to comply with, for example, the Electronic Commerce Directive can either be dealt with in section 4.3 above – by identifying the person required to sign-off a document – or in a separate document. The latter option is probably better.*]

6. Security and content management

6.1 Website security forms part of our overall information security policy which can be found at [*location of policy*].

6.2 Resources for guidance, training and support in information security, including website security, are available to all staff at [*location of guidance, etc.*]. Please contact [*name/role and contact details*] for help and advice. To report a security incident please contact [*name/role and contact details*] or in an emergency or after business hours contact [*name/role and contact details*].

7. Annual review

7.1 This policy will be reviewed annually on [*date*] by [*name of relevant member in senior management team*] as part of the annual review of the information management system.

7.2 If you have any suggestions for how this policy could be improved please contact [*name and contact details of relevant member in senior management team or delegate*].

8. Privacy compliance

8.1 The website shall have a full privacy policy clearly accessible for a user from the homepage, detailing how data from visitors to the site is used, processed, stored and deleted. For a full worked example of a privacy policy please see the Information Commissioner's website at **ico.org.uk/global/privacy-notice**.

8.2 The website will have a full cookie notice outlining all of the cookies in use on the site, what purpose they fulfil, what data they harvest, what that data is used for and how long the cookie remains present on the user's device. For a full worked example of a cookie notice please see the Information Commissioner's website at **ico.org.uk/global/cookies**.

8.3 The website shall have a full set of user Terms of Use detailing in full the rights and responsibilities of the firm via the site to the user, the limitations of these rights and any rights that the user has to rely on the website and its contents.

8.4 On the homepage, the website must also carry the full name of the registered law firm along with confirmation that the firm is authorised and regulated by the SRA (in a similar manner to how this must also be recorded on a firm's hardcopy letterhead).

Annex 8C

Electronic backup and recovery system checklist

1. The system for electronic backup and recovery must be able to ensure business continuity of the firm in the event that there is any loss of data, or corruption of data, within the firm's online systems.
2. The system must work:
   - in the event of a cyber attack; and
   - in the event of a wider infrastructure failure (e.g. total power cut, natural disaster damaging the offices, etc.).
3. The system must include two distinct and separate locations where the backup data will be stored.
5. Any backup system should be rigorously tested every three months.
6. The tests must ensure that:
   - a full system reset and restore is possible; and
   - individual files or records can be restored in isolation.
7. A complementary system must be in place to divert the phones and to notify staff in the event that the offices cannot be accessed.

Annex 8D

Device destruction protocol

Best practice when destroying obsolete IT hardware (PCs, telephones, laptops, tablets, etc.) includes the following:

1. An individual destruction certificate must be obtained for each and every piece of data-storing equipment that is destroyed.
2. Under no circumstances should the firm accept just one certificate to cover a batch of devices.

[*Add the following points if a third-party contractor is appointed to handle the destruction of the firm's IT hardware.*]

3. The third-party contractor must either destroy equipment onsite or provide audio-visual confirmation of the destruction of hardware.
4. The third-party contractor must confirm that they have previous experience in destroying IT hardware for other professional firms.
5. Any member of staff from the third-party contractor must be accompanied at all times by firm staff while onsite at the firm. Contract staff must not be unaccompanied at any time while on the firm premises (including front-of-house or back-office locations).

9 Cyber security solutions – personnel

No cyber security countermeasures will be effective unless all the staff are aware of the risks that their organisation faces from cyber security attacks; the staff must all work together to ensure that threat is minimised as much as possible.

The following chapter suggests a range of practical steps that could be included in a business's cyber security policies, but should also serve as a starting point for the reader to think in a more focused way about what areas need most attention in their organisation.

9.1 Cyber security within the office

Within the office, it is essential to maintain day-to-day cyber security awareness and establish a culture of thoroughness and care; lax attitudes, or any cutting of corners with regards to security, should not be allowed to persist.

9.1.1 General office information management

There can be inherent information security risks within the workplace; sensitive information can be:

- left on the whiteboards in meeting rooms;
- left on presentation systems where a set of slides could be left on a third-party desktop;
- left on a USB drive connected to a projector system;
- left on a flip chart;
- left on leftover copies of notes or slides left in a room after a meeting has concluded;
- overheard if doors and windows are left open;
- recorded or streamed by attendees on mobile devices.

Always ensure that all information is removed from a meeting room or venue after the meeting has concluded.

9.1.2 Password security

Staff often share passwords to machines, systems and accounts due to convenience, and because they have confidence in their colleagues. However, this practice should be discouraged, along with leaving passwords in hardcopy form where they can easily be found, such as on Post-its either attached to or adjacent to devices.

You might like to investigate password management software, to help you manage your passwords securely.

Action point – Training on passwords

The majority of systems require the use of a password, and too often staff will use either a password that is simple to hack or the same password across multiple accounts.

The most common password in the world is just that – 'password' – along with simple variations such as 'password1' and '123456'. These passwords will be cracked very simply and easily by an experienced cyber criminal.

Many firms invest in systems which require passwords to be entered on multiple levels (for example, when logging onto a machine, then again before accessing email or a virtual private network (VPN), and then again before accessing a case management system). The integrity of these multiple-level systems is destroyed if the same password is used across all of them by the same user, which frequently happens.

Staff should be given help and guidance in sound password management. Ideally passwords should be at least 10 characters in length, use a mixture of numbers and upper and lower case characters, and include non-alpha numeric characters such as '@', '#' or other symbols. Finally, these passwords should be regularly changed, so that at a minimum of every three months passwords are reset to something identifiably different.

A frequent complaint from employees is that passwords get in the way and also become difficult to remember. Encourage the adoption of loose 'systems' that are easy and memorable to staff to follow. If there is a popular local sports team, they will have a squad made up of players' names and shirt numbers for each season, already giving a start with a surname and a short number that can be incorporated into a password. Failing that, passwords could be created themed around a charity that a firm supports, or other interests or hobbies held by the staff. The key is not to use a theme that is too obvious – e.g. passwords based on an office address or the name of a partner or director. An experienced hacker would easily crack a password system based on such a clear connection to the firm.

9.1.3 Device security

An unlocked computer in the workplace could lead to unauthorised access. If the machine is locked it helps to protect data and safeguards staff from blame if the machine is misused while they are away from their desk. Computers and other work-related devices should be locked whenever they are left unattended, even if it's just for a few minutes. This is important when working in the office, but absolutely essential when working remotely. In 2016, a photo of a laptop open with the screen unlocked and left unattended on a table in a first-class train carriage went as viral as it is possible for an image to go on LinkedIn after it was shared online as an example of poor device and information management.

Ensure that devices are always kept securely and that they can be accounted for at all times. We have all heard stories in the press of laptops or tablets being left on trains, in taxis or at the back of a bus, forgotten by their owners. USB drives are easily lost – but despite being small enough to fall out of pockets, they can often contain the equivalent of five filing cabinets of data, and should be treated with due care and attention. Devices can be stolen from vehicles, left on the back seat or in the car boot while the vehicle sits in the user's very own driveway. These examples may seem obvious, but the ICO continues to fine organisations for losses of data due to these sorts of simple mistakes, so ensure that staff are fully aware of the importance of protecting such devices. If any member of staff considers the necessary precautions onerous or an unwanted burden, invite the member of staff to surrender the device and work solely from the secure office environment rather than create an unwarranted risk.

9.1.4 Desk security

If staff have messy desks, sensitive information is more likely to be left out and less likely to be noticed if it goes missing. Files should be stored in lockable filing cabinets, not left out overnight. If possible, instigate a clear desk policy so no confidential or privileged information is left on a desk when the member of staff is out of the office. Such information should be removed from workspaces and should not be visible to cleaning staff, security staff, caretakers or any other external contractors present in the office.

9.1.5 Data retention

Retaining data for longer than is necessary, often unknowingly, is one of the most common ways law firms breach the Data Protection Act (DPA) 1998. It can also lead to significant IT costs and an unacceptable risk to cyber security. Under DPA 1998, personal data should only be used for the specific reason for which it has been acquired and should be destroyed once it is no longer required, ensuring that it is not stored for longer than is necessary. In practice, this usually means that law firms store their hardcopy client files for six years before having them destroyed in line with statutory limitation. However, often firms simply destroy their files for reasons of space and cost, not knowing that they should also be doing it for reasons of compliance with DPA 1998.

The same principles apply to data that is used and stored online. Some law firms have whole servers storing years of emails. However, these emails (particularly those with attachments where clients may have supplied additional personal data) should only be stored for as long as is necessary. Again, six years would be a suitable cut-off point. After that time, it would be reasonable for all emails to be deleted. Otherwise, it would be a clear cyber security risk, with confidential and likely legally privileged communication at risk of being hacked by an unscrupulous third party, as well as a breach of DPA 1998.

In one instance I advised an organisation after an unknown member of staff had knowingly accessed client-related personal data that should have been destroyed years ago. The employee deliberately forwarded the data to the actual named data subject, which led to the organisation becoming involved in a clear data protection breach that had to be reported to the Information Commissioner. This was knowingly and maliciously done by the employee to create problems for the organisation in a way that was not easy to find but would cause maximum embarrassment and financial loss to the organisation. During that investigation it quickly became apparent that the organisation was not destroying its unnecessary records on a regular basis and the severity of the breach increased accordingly.

Therefore, personal data that is being stored online must be reviewed and deleted, just as hardcopy records must be reviewed and deleted. This should have the welcome effect of creating more storage space as records are destroyed, or reducing storage costs if the data is being hosted online in the cloud.

Retention of CCTV footage

CCTV footage contains personal data as the images they record, along with any sound, would constitute personal data if they allow an individual to be identified.

Some systems allow for electronic video recordings to be backed up online for months, if not years. Given that CCTV is generally required just for security reasons and to confirm who is in the building at a certain date or time, it should not be necessary to retain it for six years. In fact, keeping it for longer than six days is probably unnecessary without a good specific reason. Many analogue systems used to write over their tape-based storage after a few hours or days, but with the onset of digital systems, and comparatively cheap unlimited storage, many organisations are now recording high quality HD footage of their offices and storing it indefinitely – without even realising it. One organisation was fined by the ICO after the server storing its CCTV footage was hacked. Years' worth of CCTV footage was found to have been kept on a unsecured, unencrypted server without any real knowledge or awareness by the management.

9.1.6 Device destruction

All electronic devices – from desktop PCs, laptops and tablets all the way through to Blackberries and smartphones – should be destroyed. Full records of that destruction must be retained in order to prove that secure destruction has taken place.

Too many organisations forget to include all mobile devices in this exercise. It can be tempting to bequeath devices to family members after the firm has finished with them, or donate unwanted devices to a charitable organisation that reconditions old electronic equipment for schools. But anything other than official destruction is a risk and can lead unknowingly to a cyber security breach.

9.1.7 Registering as a data controller with the ICO

All law firms (and indeed the majority of private organisations employing staff or holding personal data for any other reason) should be registered as data controllers on the ICO's register. A surprisingly large amount of law firms are not registered with the ICO, despite it being a requirement under DPA 1998 and in turn a requirement of the SRA for law firms.

Registering is relatively straightforward – firms must complete a short registration form and pay a small fee – yet many firms have not done so. The ICO has indicated that increasingly punitive measures will be taken against organisations that should have registered and have not done so, and organisations that do not regularly renew their registration as necessary. In 2015 the ICO issued the first fines to firms for failure to renew their registration details; organisations should record their renewal date and take appropriate measures to ensure that their registration does not lapse.

9.2 Cyber security outside the office

Flexible working practices are now essential for modern firms wanting to increase productivity and attract the best staff. However, if legal work is being undertaken – with the use of confidential client, commercially confidential or legally privileged information – the methods for working remotely must be as cyber secure as possible.

9.2.1 Remote working outside the office

Information becomes more vulnerable when work is done outside of the normal office or workspace. Extra care should be taken to avoid any unnecessary risks. Points to be aware of when working on the move include:

- Be vigilant of any mobile devices. Make sure the screen of your laptop (or smartphone, tablet, etc.) is not visible to others.
- Check before you leave that you haven't forgotten anything. In particular, be aware of leaving behind USB drives, documents or a mobile device. *Always* double-check.
- Avoid discussing sensitive details in places where others may overhear. Pay attention to who is around you and within earshot.
- Work tidily and with care, ensuring no personal or confidential information is on display to be overlooked by anyone else.
- Remove your pass when you leave the workplace so that your name and office details are not available for all to see.

Remain aware of your surroundings when working outside of the office and aware of how information can be compromised. Trains, hotels, cafés and bars often offer free WiFi. Be aware that the information sent over these links can be freely available to other users on the same network and can be easily compromised. Consider the security of such services very carefully before using them to transfer any sensitive information.

9.2.2 Remote working from home

It may seem reasonable to consider working from home a much safer option than working in a public location. However, there are still significant risks that must be considered. Some key examples include:

- **Document disposal:** Don't throw any sensitive or confidential documents into the general household rubbish. Dispose of paper documents just as securely as you would in the office.
- **Insecure home networks:** Web-based email accounts are particularly risky. Avoid using personal email addresses to send confidential company information. Always check and comply with your organisation's policies. Connect to the business network using a VPN. If using a wireless network, make sure the connection is secure (a minimum of WiFi Protected Access II (WPA2)) with a good level of encryption and a suitable security key.
- **Mobile phones:** When dealing with sensitive information over the phone be aware of anyone else at home who might overhear, purposefully or not.
- **Document security:** Get into the habit of keeping personal or confidential information discreet. Don't just leave things lying around where others may be able to see them.
- **Personal IT equipment:** If personal IT equipment is being used, ensure that each device is authorised by the firm and that all devices comply with any business security requirements – e.g. ensuring that an up-to-date operating system and software is in use, that antivirus systems are up to date and that a firewall is installed.
- **Social media risk:** Use the privacy settings on social media to control what information is being shared – e.g. your location or activity, if it is work-related in any way.

Action point – Training for cyber security outside the office

Working in public places

Staff need to be aware of the risks of working in public places, in particular trains, cafés and restaurants. This can include holding meetings with colleagues or clients, or holding work-related phone conversations in public. Staff need to be aware of the usual issues surrounding client confidentiality, but also aware of office security and online security. Things like diary commitments, workloads, future movements and client-related matters should never be discussed, even if the names of clients aren't specifically referred to.

It is often forgotten that those sitting nearby may understand more than the participants realise. In the last year I've overheard conversations between lawyers about clients and court proceedings, while I have also been contacted by very upset clients of other law firms who have been appalled to hear their dealings with a law firm discussed by a table full of fee earners sat at a nearby table in a restaurant.

Information that might allow a password to be cracked or a system hacked could also be easily betrayed in such a manner.

Similarly, remind staff that mobile device screens can be observed by third parties and documents might easily be read by someone sat next to them.

Public charging points

Charging mobile devices from public electricity sockets (e.g. the types that can be found in hotels, airports, trains, etc.) is a cyber security risk. The majority of mobile devices use USB technology to charge, and more than just electricity can be transmitted to the device during charging. Malicious apps or code could be downloaded that could cause widespread damage to the device or cause personal or confidential data to be accessed and transmitted.

For staff who are frequently out of the office for work purposes it may be prudent to encourage them to only charge their devices using trusted power sources. It may also be prudent to provide such staff with their own additional portable battery pack. These are small devices that can store enough power to fully recharge a phone two or even three times, thus helping staff avoid the need to use a public power source.

Public WiFi networks

Free public WiFi networks in trains, airports hotels, etc., are increasingly common and are frequently used for business-related purposes. Even temporary conferences and events now offer delegates free WiFi. However, free WiFi networks are a major red light for those undertaking work-related activity online.

For example, a malicious user could use the network to access the devices of other users and search for personal data – particularly emails containing sensitive or financial data, and transactions such as online purchases.

Fake networks are another risk – a network might appear to be a free and open WiFi network but actually be a smartphone projecting a WiFi network through their own 3G or 4G data connection. An employee could easily access such a network, thinking they are accessing the network provided by a café but in fact accessing a network set up by a third party with the express intention of installing malware onto the devices of unsuspecting users.

As a result, the use of public WiFi networks for work-related activity should be strongly discouraged.

9.3 Personal data protection

Personal data is one an organisation's key assets. Client information, contact lists and also employee data are not only important from a business perspective but are also the main thing that cyber attackers will be looking to acquire. Personal data (defined in DPA 1998 as anything that allows an individual to be identified) should be protected like gold dust across the organisation.

Action point – Training staff to be aware

Your staff are the main line of defence against cyber security and they have to be aware of both the sensitivity of the data that they handle every day and the possible risks from what appear to be legitimate communications. Staff should:

- be able to identify a possible phishing email;
- know what to do when they spot a phishing email or other cyber security risk;
- be aware of what caller behaviours could be classed as suspicious;
- always ask a caller to the office to verify their identity;
- know what constitutes personal data and know what measures to take when using, transmitting or storing it;
- be aware of common cyber security fraud threats;
- know what is in the firm's cyber security policy;
- know how to report any cyber security risks or breaches.

9.3.1 Email security

Law firms, as any solicitor knows, love emails. Most members of staff have huge in-boxes that can never be cleared, and IT departments are forever asking for more funds as server after server is filled with hundreds of thousands of often meaningless messages. Yet ask a solicitor or partner if their email system is encrypted – and to what standard – and they will often stare back blankly. This is frequently because it is not encrypted at all, making an email as secure as a postcard delivered by hand and seen by multiple individuals. Even Google has confirmed, in a US lawsuit in June 2013, that Gmail users should not expect their messages to remain private. So although it is convenient for almost every business purpose, email should not be assumed to be safe and secure by default.

When sending external emails, always ask:

1. Does the information need to be protected?
2. Does the email need a security label?
3. Is the information personal or confidential?
4. Who is the intended recipient of the information?
5. How should the information be sent?

(If in doubt about how it should be sent, management should be consulted and the recipient may also need to be consulted for the most appropriate and secure form of delivery.)

6. What kind of protection does the email require? Encryption or recorded delivery?

See **Annex 9D** for more information on how to safely encrypt emails when sending personal, confidential, legally privileged or commercially sensitive data.

Action point – Training for phishing

Despite rigorous precautions, phishing email can still pose a significant threat. The following steps can identify a possibly fraudulent email:

- **The sender**: check the sender's email address. Do you know where the email is coming from? Do you know the individual or the organisation? Is this their usual email address? Even then, spam email can be sent from legitimate contacts if they themselves have been subject to a cyber attack. Their own system could have been compromised by malware which may have accessed their contact list, leading to your receipt of a phishing email.
- **The subject**: You should always give your emails a meaningful subject, and expect to receive emails with valid subjects as well. An out of the ordinary or poorly written subject line may hint at a fraudulent email or spam email. Does the email subject look unusual, for example using an 0 instead of an O, are there any spelling mistakes? Is there excessive punctuation?
- **Attachments**: Are there any documents attached to the email? If so, ask yourself:
- Do you recognise the attachment format? Excel, Word, PDF or JPEG files may be sent during the course of normal business, but be wary of .zip files if you are not expecting them, along with .exe files.
- Does the email mention the attachment at all? (No reference to an attachment may suggest that the attachment is malicious.)
- Are you expecting to receive an attachment from the sender? Attachments can transmit malware and should be opened with caution.
- **Content**: Fraudulent emails may state that a task detailed in the main body of the email requires 'immediate' action. This is intended to persuade the recipient to rush, so they are less likely to be cautious and more likely to reveal confidential information. The action could be to:
- visit a website;
- send personal/confidential information;
- reply to the email.

Be wary of emails that request personal information, particularly banking information. Banks and other financial institutions will never ask you to disclose confidential personal information, such as your password, in an email. Some emails may state that you need to reactivate an account due to maintenance, or that your computer contains malware and needs to be cleaned. Never respond to any such requests.

- **Links:** Be wary of links in emails. Links can easily be disguised and may take you to malicious websites where your PC could be compromised. Only click on links that take you to a clearly defined website or to content that you are expecting to receive from a trusted source. If you receive an email with attachments that you are not expecting from a sender, see if it is possible to recognise the sender and check if they have indeed sent an attachment with their email. If you receive an email from a bank or other organisation asking you to verify password information via a link, do not open it. Banks never send such emails. Attachments can be saved to folders without opening them, whereupon they can be scanned with antivirus software before opening. IT systems can also be configured to scan all files when they are opened for any possible hazards. Think before you open an email attachment.

9.3.2 Online browsing

When members of staff are using business devices to browse online, whether for personal or business reasons, the company policy on visiting sites should be adhered to at all times (see **Annex 9A**). Users should always be fully aware of the dangers posed by counterfeit websites. Sites should be considered suspicious if they have:

- a poor use of English and grammar;
- a strange web address;
- graphics and logos that appear slightly different or out of date compared to the user's expectation.

If in doubt, always leave such a site. Your system should use software that warns users:

- if they are about to visit a site that is known to be malicious; or
- if the site presents a another possible security risk (e.g. its security certificate is invalid or out of date).

9.3.3 Social media exploitation

Social media exploitation is an increasingly common form of cyber security attack. Social media users routinely share vast amounts of information online, even on networks like LinkedIn. Status updates often reveal career information, work location, a hobby, a social habit, personal data, family information or (in some instances) confidential or legally privileged information. All of this can be used both to guess possible password combinations and to target the user with an email containing a link or malicious attachment that could compromise their system.

For example, a LinkedIn user who has listed cycling as an interest could be targeted with a email containing a link to an apparent cycling forum. This link could then direct the user to a malicious website where his system could be accessed and personal or business data stolen.

For this reason staff need to be careful about the type of information that they share in profiles and status updates and also who they connect with. For example, LinkedIn users often connect with other users that they have never actually met, despite explicit guidance from LinkedIn not to do so. A verifiable and trusted introduction is acceptable, but an unsolicited connection request could be a scam and lead to the data that you are share online being exploited.

Fraudsters might also set up fake profiles purporting to be employees of a prestigious firm. Users will then accept the request under the mistaken impression that the profile is genuine and will be a useful contact. Once connected, the bogus profile will send messages requesting assistance, in order to draw the user into either providing confidential data or becoming involved in laundering money or in some way providing a legitimate face to criminal activity – without the user even being aware.

Annex 9A

Internet access policy

1. Person with overall responsibility

The person with overall responsibility for the internet access policy is [*name and job title*]. Technical questions, including requests to access blocked sites and any security issues, should be addressed to [*name or function/job title and contact details*]. In the event that they are absent or otherwise unavailable, queries should be addressed to [*name or function/job title and contact details*].

2. General approach to using the internet

[2.1 [*Name of practice*] provides you with internet access in order to enable you to access information, news and social networking sites that will assist you in carrying out your work, keeping you informed and promoting the practice. [If you intend to publish on a social networking site and can be identified as an employee of [*name of practice*] you should consult our guidelines which can be found at [*location*].]]

[OR]

[2.1 Internet facilities should only be used where you have [*the explicit authority of your line manager/written authority*] to do so. Your use of any internet facilities must be in accordance with the conditions or restrictions brought to your attention at the time of authorisation and as amended from time to time. These can be found at [*location of any conditions or restrictions*].]

2.2 Internet facilities will only be available once you have received cyber security induction training and passed the accompanying assessment with an 80% pass mark. Internet facilities will be withdrawn should you proceed to miss two consecutive cyber security refresher training sessions or should you subsequently fail to attain a pass mark of 80% in a refresher assessment.

3. Permitted and prohibited use of the internet

3.1 You are permitted to make reasonable personal use of the internet during working hours. Staff are expected to use their discretion in doing so. [*This should only be granted at the discretion of the firm.*]

3.2 You should not access websites that could be deemed offensive or obscene. If you inadvertently access such a site you should leave it. Failure to do so could result in disciplinary action as set out in [*location of relevant staff handbook*]. Examples of material deemed offensive by [*name of practice*] are:

- [*Examples*]

Note: The Information Commissioner's Data Protection Employment Practices Code suggests that:

'In the case of internet access, specify clearly any restrictions on material that can be viewed or copied. A simple ban on "offensive material" is unlikely to be sufficiently clear for people to know what is and is not allowed.'

It suggests providing examples of the sort of material that is considered offensive, such as material containing racist terminology or nudity.

3.3 You should take care not to download material or access internet services that could pose a threat to the security of [*name of practice's*] systems. All staff should have received training in [*title of training course*] and if you are in doubt you should consult [*name, job title and contact details*].

3.4 You should not enter into a contract or purchase goods and services on behalf of [*name of practice*] on the internet. Further information on this topic is available at [*location of guidance and/or a training course*].

3.5 You should avoid downloading any material that may be protected by copyright unless you are entitled to do so. Further information can be found at [*location of guidance and/or a training course*]. Examples could include images taken from Google Images for use in a presentation, or downloaded audio/video recordings.

3.6 You are not permitted to view the following websites while on the firm's internet services – access to these sites will remain blocked:

- [*List sites such as social media sites (e.g. Facebook, Twitter, etc.) webmail (e.g. Yahoo, Gmail, etc.) or cloud storage sites (e.g. Dropbox).*]

4. Monitoring of internet use

4.1 [*Name of practice*] monitors staff internet use and keeps a record of each website you visit and the duration of your visit. This monitoring is conducted for the purpose of [*explain the purpose of the monitoring*]. The monitoring covers [*explain the extent of the monitoring*] and it is carried out by means of [*explain how the monitoring is carried out*].

5. Internet management and security

5.1 [*Name of practice*] uses tools to automatically block access to certain websites and to automatically monitor its systems to prevent security breaches. If you need to access a website that has been blocked you should contact [*name, job title and contact details*]. You may be asked to explain why you need access to the blocked website.

6. Annual review

6.1 This policy will be reviewed annually on [*date*] by [*name of relevant member in senior management team*] as part of the annual review of the information management system.

6.2 If you have any suggestions for how this policy could be improved please contact [*name and contact details of relevant member in senior management team or delegate*].

This policy applies to internet access on PCs and mobile devices provided by the firm and shall be observed at all times.

Annex 9B

Password security protocol

Password strength suggestions

Three strong options

1. Minimum of 8 characters, with a mix of number, upper and lower case letters, and non-alphanumeric characters (e.g. #,&,@).
2. Phrases (if long passwords are permitted). For example, 'theywerethebest oftimestheywereth eworstoftimes'.
3. Three random words together. For example, ChickenPatioTulip.

How to choose and remember multiple/changing passwords

Option 1

Base your passwords around one theme and one format, but regularly change the specific details. Two examples are given below:

- **Theme:** Fantasy football team (eleven players and a manager gives twelve names – one for each month).

  Format: Player's name with jersey number (e.g. 'RobsonKanu9', 'Ledley16').

Or

- **Theme:** Holidays

  Format: Numerical month with location and currency (e.g. '06Florida$$', '08Tokyo¥¥').

Option 2

Use a quote-of-the-day app or a calendar to inspire your passwords, and include the date of the quote as well A paper calendar works best as you can make a mark on the day or tear out the quote to remind you but it just looks like you like the quote, not that it is a password (e.g. 'DoNotGoGentle05', 'CallMeIshmael23'.

Option 3

Pick three items that you can see from your desk, window or on your way to and from work that are unconnected but will serve to remind you of your current password (e.g. 'CoatstandBulldogCourt', 'TubeCafeTunnel'.

General guidelines

- Passwords must be changed *regularly*, at least every three months.
- *Do not* alternate back and forth between different passwords.
- *Do not* use the same password across multiple accounts.
- *Do not* use online password apps or password saving apps.
- Only use a password generator if you have a safe and secure way of storing and remembering the password.
- *Do not* store your password on your desk, or on your monitor.

Annex 9C

Email policy

1. **Person with overall responsibility**

   1.1 The person with overall responsibility for the email policy is [*name and job title*]. Technical questions, including security matters, should be addressed to [*name or function/job title and contact details*]. In the event that they are absent or otherwise unavailable, queries should be addressed to [*name or function/job title and contact details*].

2. **General approach to the use of email**

   2.1 [*Name of practice*] provides the following systems for business use: [*briefly outline the email and related facilities offered by the practice, e.g.*

   - *standard email facilities (e.g. Microsoft Outlook)*
   - *webmail facilities*
   - *push email facilities*
   - *encryption services*
   - *remote access to emails*
   - *facilities for sending personal emails*]

   2.2 Email facilities should only be used where you have [*the explicit authority of your line manager/written authority*] to do so. Your use of a system must be in accordance with the conditions or restrictions brought to your attention at the time of authorisation and as amended from time to time, which can be found at [*location of any conditions or restrictions*] and outlined as part of your cyber security induction training delivered on [*date of induction cyber security training*].

   2.3 Staff who have been granted access to email facilities are responsible for ensuring that:

   - they only use appropriate templates/system-produced drafts, or, where these are not available, that they follow the practice's style and content protocol which can be found at [*location of more detailed guidance*]; and
   - they follow the [*practice's/department's*] review and approval procedure by [*referring drafts to their line manager/following the workflow process*].

   2.4 If staff are uncertain about the correct procedure to follow they should always consult their line manager. They should never rely on their own authority.

3. **Permitted and prohibited use of email**

Personal use of email

   3.1 Staff are not permitted to use the practice's email facilities for non-business purposes.

3.2 In exceptional circumstances, you may apply to your line manager for permission to send a non-business related email. Your manager will consider this request and may make special arrangements to allow you to send such an email [*using a dedicated machine*].

3.3 [*Name of practice*] discourages the receipt of non-business related emails and you should make this clear to potential correspondents.

Avoid defamatory, offensive and obscene emails

3.4 You should never send emails that could be construed as defamatory. Further information is located at [*location of guidance and/or a training course*]. If in doubt do not send; consult your line manager.

3.5 You should never compose or distribute emails that could be construed as offensive or obscene. Examples of the sort of material that [*name of practice*] would consider offensive or obscene include:

- [*Examples*]

> **Note:** The Information Commissioner's Data Protection Employment Practices suggests that '[a] simple ban on "offensive material" is unlikely to be sufficiently clear for people to know what is and is not allowed' and recommends providing examples.

Avoid inadvertent contracts by email

3.6 It is possible to form a contract by email. You should take care not to do so. Further information on this topic is available at [*location of guidance and/or a training course*].

Avoid distributing copyright material

3.7 You should avoid downloading copyrighted material from the internet (or obtaining it from other sources) and should not distribute copyrighted material by email. Further information is available at [*location of guidance and/or a training course*].

4. Email monitoring

4.1 The firm monitors all incoming and outgoing emails. This monitoring is conducted for the purpose of [*explain the purpose of the monitoring*]. The monitoring covers [*explain the extent of the monitoring*] and it is carried out by means of [*explain how the monitoring is carried out*].

5. Email management and security

5.1 You are responsible for the security of the emails you send. Resources for guidance, training and support in information security, including email security, are available to all staff at [*location of guidance, etc.*]. Please contact [*name/role and contact details*] for help and advice. To report a security incident please contact [*name/role and contact details*] or in emergencies or outside business hours contact [*name/role and contact details*].

6. **Annual review**

   6.1 This policy will be reviewed annually on [*date*] by [*name of relevant member in senior management team*] as part of the annual review of the information management system.

   6.2 If you have any suggestions for how this policy could be improved please contact [*name and contact details of relevant member in senior management team or delegate*].

7. **Personal/confidential/commercially sensitive data**

   7.1 Personal data (defined as any data that allows an individual to be identified, including – in addition to names, addresses, ID, bank account information, date of birth, national insurance numbers, email addresses and phone numbers – media such as video footage and audio recordings) must not be sent via email that is unencrypted on an end-to-end basis.

   7.2 Personal data can be contained in legal documents including wills, property reports, copies of ID, bank statements, insurance papers, estate records, etc. Documents of this type must on no account be sent via unencrypted email.

   7.3 All personal data, along with any data of a confidential or commercially sensitive nature, should always be sent in accordance with the email and personal data encryption protocol which can be found at [*location of protocol*].

   7.4 Great care should be taken to ensure clients do not email the firm material containing personal, confidential or commercially sensitive data. Such material should not be sent to the firm via the client's own unencrypted email but via other more secure means including Royal Mail Special Delivery, courier or in person.

Annex 9D

Email and personal data encryption protocol

- Personal data should *never* be sent via unencrypted email.
- Never refer to personal data, including bank account details, in the body of an email.
- Any attachments (such as draft wills, property reports, medical reports, etc.) containing personal data should always be encrypted.

In the absence of standard encryption programs (e.g. Secure Sockets Layer (SSL), Gnu Privacy Guard (GPG), etc.) to encrypt your email end-to-end (i.e. not just encrypted on your email server but during transmission as well), consider using a free encryption package such as 7-Zip (**www.7-zip.org**). This will allow any attachments to be encrypted and a password to be applied.

The basic steps for using 7-Zip are:

1. Identify the attachments to be sent via email.
2. Encrypt using a password (in accordance with the firm's password security protocol which can be found at [*insert location of protocol*].
3. Test the 7-Zip encrypted archive to ensure the password has been saved correctly and that all of the items in the archive can be easily opened.
4. Attach the 7-Zip encrypted archive to the email. Ensure that the email contains no personal data in the body of the email. The email *must not* contain the password to the archive.
5. Communicate the password to the client by one of these alternative means:
    - a separate email sent from a different email address;
    - a phone call using trusted contact details;
    - secure messaging (e.g. through The Link App).

Having taken these precautions, *do not* ask the client to provide personal data via their email. They can send personal data via Royal Mail Special Delivery (or any delivery alternative that allows for tracking and guarantees delivery). Otherwise, the client could hand it in at the office in person or send it via courier.

Ideal premium solutions include a secure online data room that allows for both the firm and their clients to upload personal data that can be viewed only by authorised persons.

> **Note:** Solutions such as Dropbox, WhatsApp or Google Docs should *not be used* on any account (even if requested by a client for convenience).

Annex 9E

Remote working policy

General device use:

- Devices must be kept in line of sight at all times.
- Devices must not to be left unattended in public spaces (including cafés, restaurants, trains, airports, etc.).
- If a device is not in immediate use, the screen should be kept locked.
- Be aware of the risk of snooping and eavesdropping from other people in the vicinity.
- Ensure no one can take a photo of any sensitive information while you are working in a public place.
- Ensure business calls are not overheard in public places.

Device encryption

- Devices should be encrypted. (N.B. Just requiring a password does not mean a device is actually encrypted.)

Follow the password policy

- Always act in accordance with the firm's password security protocol which can be found at [*insert location of protocol*].

Public WiFi

- Never use public WiFi for work-related activity (especially when handling personal data of any type).
- If you cannot avoid using public WiFi, ensure that the device's WiFi settings reflect that a public network is being used and that the device's security settings are appropriate.
- Ensure that the network being used is genuinely the network being provided by the venue, with appropriate log-in and password information, and not a fraudulent network.

Publicly-provided devices

- Do not use public devices supplied in hotels, conference centres, etc. unless it is absolutely essential. They carry a high cyber security risk.
- Keep screens private (position them away from other people).
- Don't use public computers for any personal, confidential, commercially sensitive or legally privileged information.
- Use 'private browsing' where possible, never use 'remember me' or 'save information', and clear your browsing history and delete any downloads before closing the browser.

USBs

- USB drives and removable devices can be a source of malware, so should be scanned by anti-malware software before use. Many conferences etc. hand out USB sticks, but these could be infected (unbeknown to the organisers).
- Don't allow anyone to plug in an unchecked USB device into your computer, even if it is for genuine business reasons (e.g. to share information in a meeting).
- Always get the IT department to security check removable devices. Consider encrypting USBs that are used for work purposes, even if they are only used to hold presentation slides.

Working at home

- Ensure work-related devices are only used by the authorised member of staff and are not shared with family or friends.
- Devices should not be left in vehicles outside, even on driveways or in garages.
- Devices should not be left where they are visible to the public (e.g. in windows), particularly overnight.
- If a staff member is using personal home WiFi for work-related activity, they must ensure the home WiFi is password protected.
- If the home network is regularly used by family and friends, consider setting up a guest network with separate username and access codes (most modern routers have this facility).

Annex 9F

Social media policy

Statement or policy example where social media is not in use

> **Note:** If your firm does not participate in social media, you should issue a statement to highlight this policy to all staff to ensure they are aware and understand their obligations when using social media in their personal capacity. This will help mitigate the risk of staff incorrectly participating in social media on behalf of the firm. Staff should still be trained on the risks from social media exploitation on networks like LinkedIn, Facebook and Snapchat even if the firm itself has no formal social media presence.

Policy

[*Name of Firm*] does not participate in or use social media sites (e.g. Facebook, Twitter, Instagram, LinkedIn, [*insert further examples as required*], etc.). [*Name*] is responsible for reviewing the firm's participation in and use of social media in the firm, along with the firm's COLP. [He/she] must be informed of any breaches and will conduct a review of participation or use at least annually.

[*Name of Firm*] recognises that employees may wish to participate in or use social media for personal use. No employee must in any way bring the firm, its staff, its existing or prospective clients or third-party individuals/entities connected to the firm into disrepute or publish any information, particularly any confidential or sensitive information, relating to them when participating in, using or publishing content on any social media site or channel.

Any breach of these rules will be considered a disciplinary matter to be dealt with through the firm's disciplinary procedures.

Statement or policy example where social media is in use

Policy

[*Name of Firm*] uses social media to raise awareness of the firm. The social media policy supports our business objectives by [*insert description of how the objectives are supported*].

[*Name*] in [*department/unit/team*] is responsible for social media on behalf of our firm. No other employee or person is authorised to participate in the firm's social media activities without the agreement of [*name*].

[*Name of Firm*] participates in the following social media site(s): [*name(s) of site(s)*]. Information posted or viewed on social media sites may constitute published material. Therefore, reproduction of information posted or otherwise available online may only be done by [*name(s) or department/team*] who [*is/are*] delegated with authority to do this on behalf of the firm.

Employees must not act in such a way as to breach copyright or the licensing conditions of any website or computer program. Any breach of our social media rules or guidance will be considered a disciplinary matter to be dealt with through the firm's disciplinary procedures.

Scope

This policy covers all individuals working at all levels and grades, including partners, senior managers, officers, directors, employees, consultants, contractors, trainees, home workers, part-time and fixed-term employees, casual and agency staff and volunteers, collectively referred to as staff in this policy.

Third parties who have access to the firm's electronic communication systems and equipment are also required to comply with this policy.

Relevant social media

Social media is defined as a website or mobile app that allows a user to create a profile that may contain a limited amount of personal data about that user so that they may make online connections with other users forming a list of connections, with that list of connections being able to be articulated to other users and to be open and searchable, allowing for the creation of multiple networks of interconnected users.

This policy deals with the use of all forms of social media, including (though not exclusively and exhaustively):

- Facebook
- LinkedIn
- Twitter
- Instagram
- Snapchat
- WhatsApp
- YouTube
- Wikipedia
- all other social networking sites, sharing sites and all online postings, including blogs like Tumblr and WordPress.

Applicable use

The policy applies to business and personal use of social media whether:

(a) during office hours or otherwise;
(b) it is accessed using the firm's IT facilities and equipment;
(c) it is accessed using equipment belonging to members of staff.

Consequences of breach

Breaching this policy may result in disciplinary action up to and including dismissal. Disciplinary action may be taken regardless of whether the breach is committed during working hours, and regardless of whether the firm's equipment or facilities are used for the purpose of committing the breach.

Any member of staff suspected of committing a breach of this policy will be required to co-operate with the firm's investigation.

Staff may be required to remove internet postings which are deemed to constitute a breach of this policy, and failure to comply with such a request may in itself result in disciplinary action.

[*Name*] has the responsibility for ensuring that any person who may be involved with administration or investigations carried out under this policy receives regular and appropriate training to assist them with these duties.

Responsibility for implementation

[*Name*] has overall responsibility for the effective operation of this policy, but has delegated day-to-day responsibility for its operation to [*name*]. Responsibility for monitoring the operation of this policy lies with [*name*].

Questions regarding the content or application of this policy should be directed to [*name*].

All partners and managers have a responsibility to maintain compliance with this policy by ensuring that all members of staff understand the standards of behaviour expected of them, and by taking action when behaviour falls below what is required. Relevant training will be provided to enable individuals to do this.

Every member of staff has a responsibility to comply with this policy and must ensure that they take the time to read and understand it.

Any misuse of social media should be reported to [*name*].

Compliance with related policies and agreements – prohibited use and content

Social media should never be used in a way that breaches any of the firm's policies. If an internet post were to breach any of the firm's policies in another forum, it would also breach them in an online forum. For example, partners and staff are prohibited from using social media to:

- breach the firm's electronic information and communications systems policy;
- breach the firm's obligations with respect to the rules of relevant regulatory bodies;
- breach any obligations they may have relating to confidentiality;
- breach the firm's disciplinary rules;
- defame or disparage the firm or its affiliates, clients, business partners, suppliers, vendors or other stakeholders;
- harass or bully other staff in any way;
- breach the firm's anti-harassment and bullying policy;
- unlawfully discriminate against other staff or third parties;
- breach the firm's equality and diversity policy;
- breach the firm's data protection policy (for example, by disclosing personal information about a colleague online);
- breach any other laws or ethical standards (for example, using social media in a false or misleading way, such as by claiming to be someone other than themselves or by making misleading statements);
- provide references for other individuals on social or professional networking sites, because such references, either positive or negative, can be attributed to the firm, and create legal liability for both the author of the reference and the firm.

Breaches of any of the above policies will be subject to disciplinary action up to and including termination of employment.

Procedure for the business use of social media

Anyone who is required to use social media on behalf of the firm must seek approval for such communication from [*name*], who will ensure that the following conditions are met:

(a) The communication has been approved by the appropriate head of department.
(b) Client confidentiality is maintained.
(c) Any information relating to the firm is accurate, and can be used without breaching or jeopardising the firm's ability to maintain the confidentiality of its strategic and business information.
(d) The firm's logo, brand and/or colour scheme(s) is/are used in compliance with firm-wide protocols for their use.
(e) The SRA Code of Conduct 2011 and all legislative and regulatory requirements and restrictions are complied with.

The firm will ensure that individuals who are authorised to use social media on its behalf are trained to do so.

Anyone who is contacted for comments about the firm with a view to publication anywhere, including in any social media outlet, must direct the enquiry to [*name*] and only act in accordance with [*his/her*] subsequent instructions.

Use of social media in recruitment

> **Note:** Delete whichever of the two alternatives given below does not apply.

[The firm may use internet searches to perform due diligence on candidates in the course of recruitment. Where this is done, the firm will act in accordance with its data protection and equality and diversity obligations.]

[OR]

[The firm does not permit the use of internet searches for recruitment purposes.]

Personal use of social media

[*Firm name*] recognises that employees may wish to participate in or use social media for personal use. No employee must in any way bring the firm, its staff, its existing or prospective clients or third-party individuals/entities connected to the firm into disrepute or publish any information, particularly anything confidential or sensitive, relating to them when participating in, using or publishing content on any social media site or channel.

Any breach of our social media rules or guidance will be considered a disciplinary matter to be dealt with through our disciplinary procedures.

General prohibitions

1. Staff are not to use WhatsApp or other text messaging apps to discuss work-related matters with other members of staff or as a form of communication with clients.
2. Staff are not to stream live footage from within the workplace using live streaming apps such as Periscope, or make a broadcast of any sort, unless for a specific marketing or business promotion that has been signed off by the controller of this policy [*insert staff member's name here*].
3. Photographs or video footage of workspaces including desks, computer equipment, client files, name badges, security tags, post or personal effects are strictly forbidden.
4. Staff should not use their own personal mobile devices during working hours. Staff are expressly asked not to use their own personal mobile devices for activities including online gaming or gambling, or for the streaming of video clips or television footage including television programmes or live sports coverage.
5. Staff may not use social media to share any business-related files, documents, images or business material of any sort.

The above prohibitions have been set in order to protect the business and to protect staff. Should a member of staff have a compelling reason to challenge any of these prohibitions they should make a full business case for any efficiency, marketing or commercial benefit they have identified through the use of a specific social media platform along with an analysis of the applicable laws and any relevant regulatory governance for consideration by the controller of this policy [*insert name of member of staff here*]. The firm reserves the right to maintain or extend these general social media prohibitions in any circumstances.

Responsible use of social media

Given below are common sense guidelines and recommendations for using social media responsibly and safely.

1. Protecting the firm's business reputation:
   (a) Staff must not post disparaging or defamatory statements about:
   - the firm;
   - the firm's clients;
   - suppliers and vendors;
   - other affiliates and stakeholders.

   (b) Staff must avoid social media communications that might be misconstrued in a way that could damage the firm's business reputation, even indirectly.
   (c) Staff must make it clear in social media postings that they are speaking on their own behalf; write in the first person; and use a personal email address when communicating via social media.
   (d) Staff are personally responsible for what they communicate in social media, and should remember that what they publish might remain available for reading for a long time by anyone, including people inside or outside of the firm, future employers and social acquaintances.
   (e) If any social media communication discloses affiliation as an employee of the firm, individuals must make it clear that their views do not represent those of the firm. The following phrase must be inserted at the beginning of the communication:
   'The views in this posting do not represent the views of my employer.'
   Individuals must also ensure that their profiles and any content they post convey an image similar to that presented to clients and colleagues.
   (f) Comments about sensitive business-related topics, such as the performance of the firm, must not be posted even if it is made clear that the individual's views on such topics do not represent those of the firm. They could still damage the firm's reputation.
   (g) Any uncertainty or concern about the appropriateness of any statement or posting must be discussed with [*name*] prior to use.
   (h) If a member of staff sees content in a social media posting that disparages or reflects poorly on the firm or the firm's stakeholders, they should contact [*name*]. Everyone is responsible for protecting the firm's business reputation.

2. Respecting intellectual property and confidential information:
   (a) Staff must not do anything to jeopardise the firm's business and other confidential information and intellectual property through the use of social media.
   (b) Staff must avoid misappropriating or infringing the intellectual property of other companies and individuals, which can create liabilities for the firm, as well as the individual author.
   (c) Staff must not use the firm's logos, brand names, slogans or other trademarks, or post any of the firm's confidential or proprietary information without prior written permission.
   (d) In order to protect individuals and the firm against liability for copyright infringement, where appropriate, sources of particular information posted or uploaded must be accurately cited. If there are any questions about whether a particular post, photograph, video, audio recording or other upload might violate copyright or a trademark, [*name*] must be consulted before making the communication.
   (e) [*Staff are not permitted to add business contacts that have been made during the course of their employment to personal social networking accounts, such as Facebook or LinkedIn accounts.*]

   [**OR**]

   (e) [*The contact details of business acquaintances made during the course of employment are regarded as the firm's confidential information, and as such, individuals will be required to delete all such details from their personal social networking accounts upon termination of employment.*]

> **Note:** Delete whichever of the two alternatives given above does not apply.

3. Respecting colleagues, clients, partners and suppliers:
   (a) Individuals must not post anything:
      (i) that colleagues or the firm's customers, clients, business partners, suppliers, vendors or other stakeholders would find offensive, including discriminatory comments, insults or obscenities;
      (ii) relating to colleagues or the firm's clients, business partners, suppliers, vendors or other stakeholders without their written permission.
4. Respecting competitors and the legal profession:
   (a) Staff must not post any content on social media that could be construed as being defamatory or predatory or disparaging in any way about any other law firm or provider of legal services or its staff.
   (b) Staff must remember that this firm along with staff at other law firms represent the legal profession in England and Wales to the general public and that their behaviour on social media could be construed as denigrating not just themselves and this firm but also the reputation and standing of the legal profession as a whole.

(c) Staff should not make comments or remarks on social media or post any content that could in any way be interpreted by a member of the public as providing legal advice.

5. Social media exploitation:

   (a) Staff should on no account accept a connection request from any contact on social media that they have no prior experience or dealings with. Connection requests on LinkedIn or Facebook in particular can be from 'bogus' profiles with fake photographs. Fraudulent profiles can be used to connect with staff in order to send spam social media messages or spam emails or to obtain the personal data of a member of staff in order to facilitate a cyber security attack on that individual or the firm.
   (b) Should any member of staff receive a connection request from a contact that appears to be worthwhile and legitimate, the profile requesting the connection will be examined by the person controlling this policy before permission to proceed with the connection is given.

Monitoring of use

The firm reserves the right to monitor, intercept and review staff activity on the firm's IT systems – including, but not limited to, social media postings. This monitoring will be carried out periodically, but without notice, in order to ensure that this policy is being complied with, and for legitimate business purposes. Such access will be in accordance with the necessary laws and regulatory guidance as applicable.

Members of staff must not use the firm's IT systems for any matter that they wish to be kept private or confidential from the firm.

Monitoring and review of this policy

[*Name*] will review this policy at least annually to ensure that it:

(a) meets legal requirements;
(b) reflects best practice; and
(c) is in effective use throughout the firm.

Staff are invited to comment on this policy, and to suggest ways in which it might be improved, by contacting [*name*].

Annex 9G

Social media pledge

I understand and appreciate the impact my use of social media can have on the firm. The risk of regulatory breach, cyber security attacks and harm to personal and professional reputation caused by my use of social media on firm devices, or misuse of any social media in general, could lead to disciplinary action up to and including immediate termination. Therefore I pledge to:

1. not access personal social media accounts on firm devices (including mobile phones and tablets) unless given express written permission to do so;
2. avoid adding people to my professional networks who I do not know or who haven't been introduced to me through an existing contact;
3. never discuss work on personal social media accounts – especially with regards to clients and, co-workers;
4. only post events, accomplishments or newsworthy items generated from within the firm specifically for distribution outside the firm (e.g. charity events, training courses, award recipients);
5. never post my location using social media in a way that could identify a client;
6. never use collaborative social media such as WhatsApp, Slack or Google Docs or any other social network for work-related purposes (even if it may seem convenient);
7. immediately refer any client or third-party requests to use social media to communicate or provide instructions, documents or other information to a line manager for express written permission to be granted for its use and not to use it until such permission has been expressly granted.

PART III

Managing a cyber security breach

10 Reporting and response procedures

A firm should always have a rehearsed plan in place for how to respond to a cyber security breach. An incident room should be set up, with adequate resources in terms of hardware and staff, and a clear timeline should be set out detailing the approved step-by-step strategy for responding effectively at a time of crisis.

It is essential that in the immediate aftermath of the incident you do everything that you can to contain the situation. This means engaging with the key organisations without delay in order to limit the damage and bring about the best possible result in rectifying it. Remember that operating a compromised client account could be regarded as a breach of trust and may also constitute serious misconduct because of the impact on clients.

10.1 Reporting a cyber attack

Once a breach has been identified, it will be necessary to identify the size of the breach, stop it from happening again, notify those affected (including insurers), confirm what has happened to staff, and control the flow of information. Even for the smallest of firms, it may be necessary to put out a short press release and statement on the firm's website to answer any queries from concerned clients, third parties and suppliers while the investigation remains ongoing.

In the event of a cyber security breach, would your staff know how and when reporting should take place? The list below should give you actions to consider *but should not be considered exhaustive.*

10.1.1 The SRA

Regardless of whether you think the attack – and any subsequent loss of data – constitutes a material or non-material breach, it is advisable to contact the SRA, who will give further guidance on the severity of the breach. Depending on the severity, the attack may need to be reported outside of your firm's regular breach-reporting procedure, and may require immediate notification.

To inform the SRA call 0121 329 6827 or email fraud@sra.org.uk.

10.1.2 The police

If any sensitive data has been stolen or fraudulently accessed – particularly personal data or third-party information such as records relating to clients or suppliers – it would be prudent to report the matter to the police.

If the firm intends to make a claim on their professional indemnity insurance (PII) or cyber security insurance, a crime reference number from the police will probably be required anyway.

The police in your region will have contact numbers for non-emergency reporting of such cyber and business-related crime, so do not dial 999 unless:

- the attack is particularly large;
- the attack is ongoing;
- the attack involves the direct theft or misappropriation of funds; or
- the identity of those responsible is known and there is a strong possibility of being able to apprehend them if immediate action is taken by the appropriate law enforcement agency.

You must inform the police straight away if your client account has been compromised. To report the incident and to receive a police crime reference number, contact Action Fraud – the national fraud and cyber crime reporting centre – on 0300 123 2040, or via the business section of its website (**www.actionfraud.police.uk/BRT**).

10.1.3 The Information Commissioner's Office

If any personal data has been lost or compromised, the Information Commissioner's Office (ICO) should be notified. They may or may not wish to investigate the matter fully – in many instances they will simply ask for updates on the outcome of any investigation and will only want to take further steps if there appears to be a serious regulatory breach by the data controller. Even then, they often prefer to act only if there is a pattern of behaviour with multiple breaches over a period of months or years.

However, if a cyber attack and subsequent loss of personal data is suppressed by a data controller and then the ICO is notified by someone whose data has been lost or compromised, or notified by some other third party who has identified and confirmed the loss, the ICO will be more likely to investigate and take regulatory action. The ICO has the power to levy fines of up to £500,000 against the data controller.

10.1.4 Cyber security insurer

If your firm has cyber security insurance in place it will be necessary to initiate a claim against this policy. Early notification will be paramount so the insurer can monitor the situation. Any unreasonable delay could lead to the policy terms not being met and no payment being made. Ensure that your firm is fully aware of the terms that must be met under any cyber insurance policy that has been taken out to ensure that the benefit of having the policy is not lost.

10.1.5 Partners

As stakeholders in the business, partners or directors (or investors if your organisation is an alternative business structure (ABS)) will need to be notified of a cyber security breach because it could have a material impact on the operation and value of the business. A cyber security breach could lead to the directors being in breach of their duties under the Companies Act 2006. The directors will also be responsible for any regulatory action that may be taken against the firm.

10.1.6 Suppliers

Depending on the nature of the cyber security breach, other suppliers of online systems to the firm may also need to be notified so that they can carry out their own investigations to ensure that their systems have not been compromised as a result of the breach sustained by your firm.

10.1.7 Your bank

Contact your bank immediately if you suspect there has been an unauthorised or suspicious withdrawal from your client account. Delays in contacting the bank could lead to further loss of funds from the client account and reduce the opportunities to make recoveries. Ask your bank's relationship manager and its fraud department to help you contain the losses, secure and protect the account and records, and assist where possible in the recovery of funds taken through criminal activity.

While each bank may react differently and according to the individual circumstances, your bank can be expected to immediately freeze the client account to prevent further losses. The bank can also be expected to contact the receiving bank without delay to attempt to recover lost money, if the fraudsters have not yet taken it out from the receiving bank account.

Passwords or security with your bank may need to be changed if there is any possibility that the firm's internet or telephone banking security has been compromised. Only trusted and previously verified and secure contact information should be used when reporting such matters to your bank.

10.1.8 Your PII

Under the terms of your PII policy, you must inform your insurer of any claims or circumstances that may give rise to a claim. Loss sustained to the client account triggers a claim under your PII policy.

When notifying insurers of the claim, you should also consider your duty of client confidentiality. Client confidentiality and legal privilege can only be waived with the express consent of the client. As a precaution, in order to expedite a claim in the event of being scammed, consider adding to your terms of engagement wording to the effect that, if the firm has to make a notification under the terms of its PII policy, information about the client may be seen by your insurers. Your files may, therefore, be seen by an assessor or another person unconnected with the firm in the future, unless the client has notified you that they do not agree to this.

Depending on the policy wording, your PI insurer may need to be notified of cyber security and personal data breaches. In the event of subsequent claims for professional negligence stemming from the cyber security breach, it may serve to notify the insurer sooner rather than later.

10.1.9 Clients

Any individuals whose personal data has been compromised will have to be notified of any loss of their personal data. Depending on the nature of the data that has been lost they may have to secure their bank accounts or check for any personal data being leaked online.

10.1.10 Third parties

Any other organisation or individual whose personal data, systems or security could have been compromised as a result of a cyber security breach should be notified. These could include IT suppliers, contractors, agencies that supply staff or services, or any other organisation that your firm has regular dealings with that may be affected by the cyber security breach.

10.1.11 Staff

Regardless of whether the breach affects staff personal data (in which case the staff should definitely be informed), staff should be notified of any cyber security breach so that they can adequately deal with calls or contact from clients, suppliers or other parties. They may also need to know how to respond to enquiries from the press, police and any other agency or regulator.

10.1.12 Local/regional news

In the event of a large scale cyber security breach where significant numbers of people need to be notified, it may be prudent to consider reporting the matter to the local press to ensure that all affected parties find out and can take appropriate protective action as quickly as possible.

10.2 Incident response procedure

The precise order of urgency for your response will be dependent on your individual circumstances and what the SRA and other agencies advise, but drawing up a plan of action will help you demonstrate to the SRA, your bank and your insurer that you are acting professionally and responsibly, with serious intent to limit damage, safeguard the public interest and restore confidence in your business as a going concern.

10.2.1 Recommended steps for preparing your incident response procedure

- Assign a senior member of the firm (possibly the COLP) to take on responsibility for the plan and for integrating incident-response efforts across different departments and locations.
- Develop a classification of risks, threats and potential failure modes. Update this classification continually on the basis of changes in the threat environment.
- Develop easily accessible quick-response guides for likely scenarios.
- Ensure that documentation of response plans is available to the entire organization and is routinely refreshed.
- Establish processes for making major decisions, such as when to isolate compromised areas of the network.
- Ensure that all staff members understand their roles and responsibilities in the event of a cyber incident.
- Run simulated breaches to develop staff awareness and test their response capabilities.
- Maintain relationships with key external stakeholders, such as the SRA and the ICO.
- Maintain service-level agreements and relationships with external cyber security experts.

10.2.2 Recommended steps for implementing your incident response procedure

Cyber security firms recommend modelling your response procedure on the system used by airlines following air disasters.

- Have an incident room with appropriate staff and resources.
- Identify who is affected (e.g. clients, staff, third parties, etc.).
- Identify who needs to be notified (e.g. the police, regulators, insurers, banks, all staff, local media, etc.). This needs to be quickly decided and appropriate action taken.
- Work out a project management chart that clearly shows:
  - what actions must be taken in what order; and
  - which tasks can be carried out simultaneously and which tasks need to occur sequentially.

Action point – Training staff about the incident response procedure

- Have a clearly understood system that can be used by all members of staff if they identify a possible cyber attack. There should be clear lines of reporting that ensure that the report of an incident does not sit on one person's desk for longer than it should, and it should not pass over multiple desks more than is necessary before the COLP is notified and decisions taken and appropriate action carried out.
- The COLP should be supported in having sufficient information to identify if there has been a cyber security breach, what type of data has been affected, what volume of data is affected, and who will need to be notified as a result.
- Provide specialist training to the incident management team.

10.2.4 The aftermath

If the firm has survived and recovered, you should review the incident to see what lessons can be learnt to prevent further attacks. It is important for the firm to identify how and why the scam was successful. The firm should consider whether the scam resulted from a control failure, or whether correct preventative measures were not in place at the time.

This may involve reviewing and revising your information security, business continuity and incident response policies and procedures, as well as the firm's technical controls and systems for staff training.

10.3 Sources of help and support

10.3.1 The Law Society

The Practice Advice Service provides support for solicitors on a wide range of areas of practice and problems. The Practice Advice Service can be contacted on 0207 320 5675 or by email: practiceadvice@lawsociety.org.uk.

The Law Society has a number of useful Practice Notes, including:

- 'Protecting your firm if you fall victim to a scam' (12 April 2016); and
- 'Cloud computing' (7 April 2014).

10.3.2 The police

Action Fraud is a national police initiative, so law firms across England and Wales can benefit from this help. See **http://content.met.police.uk/Site/fraudalert** for more details.

The Metropolitan Police's FALCON (fraud and linked crime online) team are specifically highlighting the problem of 'mandate fraud' – impersonating a known contact, such as a bank or a client, and asking you to change the sort code and account number, either for making a known payment (e.g. in a conveyancing transaction) or else 'to safeguard the client account against a fraud'. As part of their prevention strategy, FALCON are also offering to meet up with firms to give best-practice advice and risk-reduction strategies.

10.3.3 The SRA

The SRA has a regularly updated section of their website that lists recently issued scam alerts – **www.sra.org.uk/alerts**.

The SRA has also published a paper titled 'Spiders in the web: The risks of online crime to legal business'.

Contact the SRA's helpline for advice on risk, systems and controls (telephone: 0370 606 2555).

10.3.4 The Information Commissioner's Office

The ICO's publication, 'Guidance on data security breach management', is a useful resource. It has also produced 'Notification of data security breaches to the ICO' and other related guidance.

10.3.5 Action Fraud

Action Fraud is the national fraud and cyber crime reporting centre. It provides information on how to report fraud and also how to report anything suspicious – e.g. a potential scam message or computer virus – that has not yet been responded to or caused any damage. Action Fraud's Business Reporting Tool enables companies to report multiple instances of fraud and internet crime more efficiently (**www.actionfraud.police.uk/BRT**).

The Action Fraud telephone number is: 0300 123 2040.

10.3.6 Cyber Incident Response (CIR) service

The government's list of certified cyber-response providers, with contact numbers, can be found on the CIR website: **www.cpni.gov.uk/advice/cyber/cir**.

Annex 10A

Breach notification (staff)

Notice to all staff

On [*date*] we experienced a cyber security breach of our systems. The cause of this breach is [*cause of breach/unknown at this time*].

[**Insert following paragraph if client data has been compromised.**]

Because this breach caused a vulnerability in our clients' personal data we are notifying all clients potentially affected. Please note that as part of this notification clients have been advised to contact their fee earner for further information. If any client contacts you regarding this letter and you have not received further information regarding this breach please refer them to [*name of person dealing with breach*]. Please also note that clients who contact you regarding this cyber security breach should on no account be charged for having contacted you or this firm.

[**Insert following paragraph if staff data has been compromised.**]

Because this breach has compromised the security of our staff data we are notifying all staff who may have been affected by this breach to take the following action:

[*delete factors as applicable depending on nature of data breached*]

- Notify your bank
- Run a credit check
- Notify your credit card providers
- Change passwords with your bank
- Check your company mobile device security
- Check the integrity and security of your social media accounts

As cyber security awareness is essential knowledge for our staff, we will be providing a supplementary training session within the next few weeks in order to educate everyone on the cause of this cyber security breach and the measures we are taking as a firm to limit the chances of such a breach happening again.

Should you have any queries regarding this cyber security breach or our cyber security policy generally please contact [*insert COLP or name of person dealing with this breach and contact info here*].

Please be assured that we taking all appropriate action to mitigate the damage from this cyber security breach and doing all that we can to safeguard your data and our client data in the future.

Yours sincerely

[*Senior partner*]

[*Direct dial contact details*]

Annex 10B

Breach notification (client)

Dear [*client name*]

As you may be aware, cyber attacks on law firms have become increasingly common in the last few years. This firm is committed to doing everything it can to limit if not eliminate cyber security breaches. Fortunately we have been able to avoid many of the common threats that have occurred within other law firms recently. Regrettably, our efforts have not been 100% successful as we have recently experienced a [*give name of type of breach*]. The systems we have in place were able to catch this intrusion quickly.

This letter is to notify you that some of your personal data may have been compromised during this attack. We are recommending that you take the following actions to ensure your personal data remains secure:

- Run a credit check
- Notify your bank
- Notify your credit card providers
- Change passwords with your bank
- Speak to your fee earner (at no cost to you)

We have also reported this breach and the fact that your personal data has been compromised to the following:

[*Add as applicable*]

- Information Commissioners Office (ICO)
- Solicitors Regulatory Authority (SRA)
- Police [*insert incident number*]
- Our professional indemnity insurer
- Our cyber insurance provider

I would like to say that I am very sorry on behalf of everyone at [*insert firm details*] that our systems have been compromised in this manner and that your data in particular has been affected.

We have taken action to rectify this weakness in our systems and have worked with our IT providers [*insert name here*], local law enforcement and specialist security consultants [*insert name here*] to ensure that we have remedied this weakness and that our firm will be a safe and reliable provider of legal services for all of our clients in the future.

As always we appreciate your business and continue to do all we can to provide you with the highest levels of service. If you have any further concerns please feel free to give me a call using the details below, or to contact our firm's compliance officer [*insert COLP name and contact details details here*]

Yours sincerely

[*Senior partner*]

[*Direct dial contact details*]

Annex 10C

Reporting a cyber security breach checklist

Use this checklist to identify if there has been a breach and what needs to be reported.

1. Does the breach involve personal data?
   If you answered 'yes' – report to ICO.
2. Does the breach constitute a material breach?
   If you answered 'yes' – report to SRA.
3. Does the breach involve client data?
   If you answered 'yes' – report to affected client(s).
4. Does the breach involve staff/HR data?
   If you answered 'yes' – report to affected staff.
5. Was the breach reported by a third party?
   If you answered 'yes' – report to your professional indemnity insurer.
6. Does the breach involve the firm's bank accounts or bank account details?
   If you answered 'yes' – notify firm's bank.
7. Does the breach involve client bank account details?
   If you answered 'yes' – notify any affected clients and the clients' banks.
8. Do you know how the system was accessed, and whether the perpetrator was external or internal?
   If you answered 'no' – consider obtaining a specialist report on how the system was accessed from a forensic IT specialist.
9. Does the breach involve fraud (e.g. scam telephone calls or phishing emails), theft of funds or theft of data?
   If you answered 'yes' – consider notifying law enforcement, ideally a police cyber-crime unit (a crime reference number may be required for certain insurance claims).
10. Do you have a specific cyber insurance policy?
    If you answered 'yes' – notify your cyber insurer.
11. Does the breach result from negligence on the part of the firm?
    If you answered 'yes' – notify your professional indemnity insurer. Your insurer should be notified in the majority of cyber security breaches, however check your policy documents.

Glossary

Adware: Something that places an advert onto your system. Some programs, when downloaded, may try to interfere with your system's web browser and redirect search requests to advertising websites. A fairly aggressive and often annoying type of advertising, but fairly benign in nature.

Air gap: Describes a device that is not connected to the internet in any way and never has been, and also has never had data entered onto it from a third-party source. Once an internet or bluetooth connection is established, or the device is exposed to third-party data, the machine is no longer air gapped and should not be referred to as such.

App: Short for 'application'; a program that fulfils a particular purpose, designed to work on tablets and smartphones.

Bit: Stands for 'binary digit', the smallest unit of information in a computer. Commonly used as a term to measure encryption, and refers to the number of bits in a memory address. So a 64-bit key takes 64 bits of computer memory.

Bring Your Own Device (BYOD): Practice in a business whereby staff work using their own devices (e.g. smartphones, tablets, etc.) rather technology provided by their employer. Often requested by staff, but contains significant security threats.

Catfishing: The practice of using an assumed identity online to trick others. The perpetrator may want to access the personal data of the victim, or to elicit a fraudulent financial transaction. Catfishing is common on social networking sites where users may find that the person they are talking to bears no resemblance to photos or material actually posted online.

Clickbait: Content, especially that of a sensational or provocative nature, that is intended to attract attention and draw visitors to a particular web page.

Cloud: Network of servers hosted by an external company (either for free or on a paid basis), and accessed via the internet.

Cookie: A small text file stored on your computer that remembers information you have entered onto certain websites (e.g. settings, search requests, etc.).

Cyber attack: A third-party attack on a system or network.

Cyber breach: A successful cyber attack leading to a network being accessed, and the leaking of personal or legally privileged data. Could also refer to the hacking of a social media account or an encrypted mobile device.

Data controller: A person who (either alone or jointly or in common with other persons) determines the purposes for which and the manner in which any personal data are, or are to be, processed.

Data processor: Any person (other than an employee of the data controller) who processes the data on behalf of the data controller.

Data subject: An individual who is the subect of personal data.

Encryption: The conversion of data into a format that can only be accessed with the correct key. Encryption keys are often measured in bits, for example, 64-bit encryption should be in place as a minimum standard on all office-based systems.

Information Commissioner's Office (ICO): The UK data protection regulator. Has the power to fine data controllers up to £500,000 for cyber security breaches involving personal data.

Internet protocol (IP): The method by which data is transferred via the internet. Every computer connected to the internet has a unique IP address.

Juice jacking: Any cyber attack implemented using a public charging port. When devices are connected to power points in a public place, the power point could have been previously tampered with, allowing malware to be installed or data stolen from the plugged-in device.

Keylogging: Using a program that logs all of the keystrokes made on a device by a user. This is one method of hacking passwords, etc.

Malvertisement: An online advert that transfers a virus or malware when you click on it.

Malware: Any software which is designed to disrupt or damage a device or computer system.

Personal data: Any information that relates to an indentifiable person. For example, name, address, national insurance number, email address, medical records, bank account details, etc.

Phishing: An unsolicited email sent to encourage the recipient to enter into a correspondence or to visit a particular website, all with the aim of accessing the personal data of the recipient or eliciting a fraudulent financial transaction. Commonly sent to law firms by fraudsters impersonating a bank or even impersonating a client.

Private network: A network that uses a private IP address. Commonly used as networks in businesses.

Remote access: Accessing a server from another location – frequently used in business to facilitate out-of-office working.

Server: A computer or device that manages network resources. There are many different types of servers. For example, a file server is a device dedicated to storing files. Your firm most likely has a server or servers in its offices or may have cloud-based servers that are not physically in the office.

Skype: Video calling service which is free to use if calling another Skype user. Can also be used for video conferencing with multiple recipients.

Social media: Websites where users have a profile and a list of connections or contacts (a network) that can be viewed by other users. Used for sharing photos, videos, music and web links, and (increasingly) for connecting with business contacts.

Trojan: A type of malware that disguises itself as a legitimate program, or conceals itself within legitimate software.

Two-factor authentication: An additional layer of security required to access a system. The basic login procedure – entering a username and password – only has one factor which verifies identity (the password). Two-factor authentication requires both a password and a second factor; for example, a code sent via text to the user's mobile phone.

USB/flash drive: A physically small device that allows for the transfer of files and data in large quantities.

Virtual private network (VPN): a private network that extends across a public network (or internet). It enables users to send and receive data across shared or public networks as if their devices were directly connected to the private network.

Web browser: Software used to access the world wide web (e.g. Internet Explorer, Safari, Chrome, etc.).

WiFi: Wireless connection to the internet, allowing access online without the need for a cable.

Useful contacts and links

The threats to your firm from cyber crime and fraud will continually evolve and develop. You may put certain steps in place to combat the current threats as a result of reading this book, but what will you do about the threats that develop as a result of new technologies and new ways of working?

It is essential that you and your firm stay up to date on the threats that are out there and best practice in combating them. This could be through a variety of ways, including:

- subscribing to networks that provide cyber security guidance;
- appointing a cyber security officer at your firm to monitor for new cyber security attacks and threats to all businesses, and UK law firms in particular, and to report back to management on a regular basis;
- attending cyber security conferences and events to identify emerging best practice.

A good place to start is the Law Society's free online course – Cyber Security for Legal and Accountancy Professionals. It counts towards your CPD, and can be found at: **cpdcentre.lawsociety.org.uk/course/6707/cyber-security-for-legal-and-accountancy-professionals**.

This course is suitable for anyone working at a law firm, regardless of seniority, and provides a general overview of the risks from cyber security and general techniques to minimise the risk.

Ultimately it will be up to you to identify a method that works best for your firm. However, I recommend the following organisations as reliable sources of up-to-date news and advice on cyber developments.

1. Governmental sources

    - Centre for the Protection of the National Infrastructure (CPNI): **www.cpni.gov.uk**
    - Cyber Essentials from the Department of Business, Innovation and Skills: **www.gov.uk/government/publications/cyber-essentials-scheme-overview**
    - Cyber Security Information Sharing Partnership (CISP): **www.cert.gov.uk/cisp**
    - Cyber Suppliers Government scheme: **www.gov.uk/government/publications/cyber-security-supplier-to-government-scheme**
    - Information Commissioner's Office (ICO): **ico.org.uk**

2. SRA sources

    - Silver Linings: cloud computing, law firms and risk (an SRA paper): **www.sra.org.uk/risk/resources/cloud-computing-law-firms-risk.page**

- Spiders in the web: the risks of online crime to legal business (an SRA paper): **www.sra.org.uk/risk/resources/online-crime-legal-business.page**

3. Law Society sources

   - Law Society Practice Notes: **www.lawsociety.org.uk/support-services/advice/practice-notes**

4. Other sources

   - British Computer Society: **www.bcs.org**
   - Cyber Streetwise: **www.cyberstreetwise.com**
     - See also Cyber Essentials (Cyber Essentials explains the basics and shows clients you are taking the threat seriously): **www.cyberstreetwise.com/cyberessentials**
   - EEMA (European think tank for e-identity and security): **www.eema.org**
   - ENISA Guide on Cloud Security: **www.enisa.europa.eu/activities/Resilience-and-CIIP/cloud-computing/security-for-smes/cloud-security-guide-for-smes**
   - Financial Conduct Authority: **www.fca.org.uk**
   - Federation of Small Business (FSB): **www.fsb.org.uk**
   - Institute of Chartered Accountants in England and Wales (ICAEW): **www.icaew.com**
   - Institute of Information Security Professionals (IISP): **www.iisp.org/imis15**
   - Society for Computers and Law: **www.scl.org/site.aspx?i=ho0**
   - Security Institute: **www.security-institute.org/home_page**
   - techUK – **www.techuk.org**
     - See also Cyber Connect: **www.techuk.org/cyber-connect-uk**
   - UK Cyber Security Forum: **www.ukcybersecurityforum.com**